Engd by J. A. O'Neill. N.Y.

RIGHT REV. S. G. BRUTE.

FIRST BISHOP OF VINCENNES, INDIANA.

MEMOIRS

OF THE RIGHT REVEREND

SIMON WM. GABRIEL BRUTÉ, D.D.,

FIRST BISHOP OF VINCENNES;

WITH

SKETCHES DESCRIBING HIS RECOLLECTIONS OF SCENES CONNECTED WITH THE

FRENCH REVOLUTION,

AND

EXTRACTS FROM HIS JOURNAL.

BY THE

RT. REV. JAMES ROOSEVELT BAYLEY, D.D.,

BISHOP OF NEWARK.

CATHOLIC PUBLICATION SOCIETY,

9 WARREN STREET.

1876.

CONTENTS.

	PAGE
Preface,	7–12
Life of Bishop Bruté,	13–106
Sketches,	108
Trial of Rev. Mr. Raoul and the Sisters,	118–123
Rev. Mr. Touchet, Rector of St. Hélier,	124–126
Death of Rev. Mr. Sorette,	127–135
Death of Rev. Mr. Duval,	136–137
The Priest and Peasant,	138–140
The Rev. Mr. Tostivint and the Marquis and Marchioness De Bedée,	141–143
The Rev. Mr. Sacquet,	144–147
The Rev. Mr. Poirier,	148–152
The Rector of Guignen and his Vicar,	153–154
The Rev. Mr. Clement,	155–158
The Death of the Rev. Mr. La Moine,	159–160
The Death of the Rev. Mr. Gautier of Brutz,	161–167
The Banishment of the Rev. Mr. Delaitre,	168–169
The Brother of the Christian Schools,	170
Father Kergaté,	171–172
Two Brothers put to death together,	173–174
Mr. Boisleve,	175–178

	PAGE
The Rev. Mr. Marechal and the Countesses De Renac,	179–188
The War in La Vendée, ...	189–192
The Prince of Rieux and Mr. Joyaux, ...	193–195
Armand de Montluc, ...	196–199
Our Sundays in 1793, ...	200–206
The Hospital of the Incurables, ...	207–212
Thirty Years, and more, ago, ...	213–215
Mr. Bouvet, ...	216–217
Journal, ...	218–261
Appendix, ...	263–269

LIST OF ILLUSTRATIONS.

1. Portrait of Bishop Bruté, engraved by O'Neill.

FROM SKETCHES BY BISHOP BRUTE.

2. Palais de Justice, Rennes, his birthplace, . . . 12
3. Cathedral, Bishop's Residence, &c., Rennes, . . face 24
4. Rev. Mr. Poirier and the Guillotine (see p. 148), . face 109
5. Rev. Mr. Raoul and the three Sisters of La Chapelle St. Aubert before the Revolutionary Tribunal, . face 120
6. The Curate of Guignen endeavouring to shield his aged Pastor from the balls of the soldiers, . . . face 154
7. Rev. Mr. Gautier of Brutz anointing in the wagon on the way to execution a countryman mortally wounded in endeavouring to save him, ... face 162
8. Rev. Mr. Clement and the Sentry (see p 115), . . . 217
9. Cathedral of St. Francis Xavier, Vincennes, . . . 262
Fig. 1 marks the site of the ancient Jesuit Chapel.

PREFACE

IT may be proper for me to state in what manner the following Papers came into my possession, and the reasons which have induced me to publish them. In 1847, Monseignor De la Hailandiere, the successor of Bishop Bruté in the See of Vincennes, presented to the Most Rev. Archbishop (then Bishop) of New York a large number of MSS. which had belonged to his predecessor. In examining them, I found amongst them a small MS. volume of Notes and reminiscences of the French Revolution, which, with the approbation of the Bishop, I determined to prepare for publication. My first idea was, to embody them in a "Life and Times of Bishop Bruté," to contain a contemporaneous History of the Catholic Church in this country, and a Selection from his extensive and valuable correspondence. In this view I collected a large number of Letters and Documents, and made many notes. But such an undertaking, as the son of Sirach says of wisdom, "cometh of opportunity of leisure," and my constant occupations then, and since, have never permitted me to carry out my design. They would probably have caused me to abandon it altogether had not some friends, to whom I had shown the Notes on the French Revolution, and who were struck with the light which they threw upon what may be called the interior or domestic scenes of that dreadful Tragedy, urged me to prepare them, at least, for publication. Having done so, I found that it was necessary to preface them by a brief Sketch of Bishop Bruté's Life. In preparing this, from the memoranda in my possession, it will be perceived that I have not attempted a Biography, properly so called, but have merely drawn out a thread of narrative to string the notes on, particularly such as illustrate the period in question. They will be found, when read in connection with the Sketches and Journal, to bring into relief a portion of the picture of the Revolution which has been too much overlooked. Historians have dwelt upon the crimes and horrors of that period, and the dark colours with which they have painted it have overlaid and hidden those scenes of Christian charity, and patience, and heroism which would have done so much to relieve the picture. The crimes of the oppressors were open and known to all men; the virtues of the sufferers were for the most part hidden, and known only to God. Even those works which were written with the intention of preserving the memory of the victims have become scarce, and are little known. I had much difficulty in obtaining a copy of the Abbé Carron's "Confessors of the Faith." I have read those which I was able to get,[1] but in none

[1] Barruel—Histoire du Clergé pendant la Révolution; 2 vol. 12mo, Londres, 1792. Carron—Les Confesseurs de la Foi dans l'Eglise Gallicane, à la fin du XVIII Siècle; Paris, 1820, 4 vol. 12mo. Walsh—Journées mémorable de la Révolution Française, par M. Le Vicomte Walsh; 5 vol. 8vo, Paris, 1840. Tresvaux—Histoire de la Persécution Révolutionnaire en Bretagne, par l'Abbé Tresvaux; Paris, 2 vol. 8vo, 1845.

of them have I found anything so fresh and homelike as the papers here published. The only regret those who read them will have, is that they are so few and brief.

It is indeed to be regretted that Bishop Bruté did not write an autobiography. His life until he came to this country was passed among the most exciting events that ever occurred—he was personally acquainted with a large number of the actors in them—his memory was strong and accurate, and he might have written a book of great historical value. His notes and memoranda show that at one time he contemplated something of the sort, but on this account they are often less useful to others, being merely hints and memoranda to assist his memory. "There is no sort of Literature," he writes in a note on "Spence's Anecdotes," "which has afforded me more pleasure than Biographies and Memoirs. I sometimes think of amusing myself by writing an account of my life. There is a quantity of anecdotes and observations which occur to me, and which if they were written down would amuse and interest my associates and friends, and might remain '*en depôt*' in the Library."

In writing his Sketches, Bishop Bruté was accustomed to illustrate the subject by drawings made with his pen. A few of these have been engraved on wood, and inserted in the work. I have selected such as are of an historical value, representing scenes which have long since passed away.

To complete the work I have also translated such portions of his Journal as are of general interest, and printed them in the Appendix. Though very brief, they are interesting as affording glimpses behind the scenes, and indicating the changes in public opinion, as the people gradually returned to their senses.

In looking over the work, now that it is finished, my only regret is, that the preparatory Biographical Sketch is not more worthy of the holy man who is the subject of it. Those who knew him, I am afraid, will be particularly disappointed at my poor *Silhouette* likeness of him. But if so, they must distribute the blame among themselves, for some one of them should, long before this, have written a Biography of one whom they remember, and so often speak of, as the model of every ecclesiastical virtue, and whose memory for piety and learning is so justly in benediction among them.

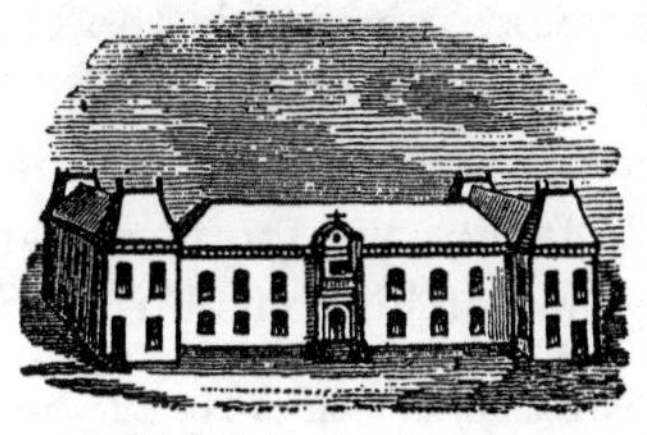

Palais de Justice, Rennes.

MEMOIRS.

THE subject of this sketch was born in Rennes, the capital of the ancient Province of Brittany, in France, on the night of the 20th of March, 1779, and was baptized [1] early the next morning in the Parish Church of St. Germain. His father, Simon William Gabriel Bruté de Remur, who belonged to an ancient and very respectable family, was born at Paris in 1729, and was at the time of his son's birth [2] Superinten-

1 Extrait du Registre concernant l'état civil de Citoyens de la ci-devant Paroisse de St. Germain de Rennes pour l'année 1779: "Simon Guillaume Gabriel, fils de Simon Guillaume Gabriel Bruté de Remur, et de Renée Jeanne Le Saulnier de Vauhelle, né et baptisé le même jour vingt mars mil septcent soixante dix-neuf. Parrain, François Pierre René Vatar de Jouanner; Marraine, Victoire Françoise Bruté de Remur, etc. Le Valler, Curé.

"Soussigné a Rennes le quatorze Thermidor, an sept de la Republique Française, une et indivisible. Dubreil."

2 His father was twice married; first to Mary Jeanne Le Chat, at Paris, the 28th February, 1756, by whom he had seven children; and, second, to Madame Vatar at Rennes in 1778, by whom he had two children, the subject of this sketch and his brother Augustine, born in 1789. "The mother of my mother, Claudienne Elienor Robert, died in 1791 aged eighty-one

dent of the royal domains in Brittany. His mother, Jeanne Renée Le Saulnier de Vauhelle, born at St. Brieux in 1736, was at the time of her marriage with Mr. Bruté the widow of Mr. Francis Vatar,[3] Printer to the King and Parliament at Rennes. Their place of residence was in the Palace of the Parliament,[4] in which his family, on the mother's side,

years. My grand-uncle, her brother Peter Robert, Prior of Etables of the order of the Prémontrés, died the 7th February, 1795, in the hospital of Guingcamp, prisoner for the Faith." *MS. Note.* Mr. Bruté's first marriage took place in the parish church of St. Eustache, and was performed by the Abbé Bruté, his uncle, Doctor in Theology and Curé of the parish of St. Benoit.

[3] "My mother has often told me that the Vatars were of English origin, and had pursued the occupation of printing since its invention in the fourteenth century. The books printed by Mr. Vatar were chiefly those on the jurisprudence of the Province, the customs, collection of ordinances, 'Les Principes du Droit' de Du Parc Pouillainge. There were 130,000 francs worth of these Books in store, when the Constituent Assembly abolished all local laws and customs, and thus entirely destroyed the value of those which my mother, who had the reversion of his title of Printer to the King and the Parliament, had on hand." *MS. Note.*

I may mention as indicating the manner in which a particular profession or occupation often continues in a family, and is handed down from father to son, in the old world, that the History of Rennes in my possession, that of De Villeneuve & Mallet, Rennes, 1845, was printed by J. M. Vatar.

[4] The fire of 1719, during the time which was made so calamitous by the System of Law, destroyed 850 houses in Rennes, a fifth of the whole city, and was considered of sufficient importance to find a place in the Abridgment of the History of France by d'Anquetil. In rebuilding that portion of the city a very beautiful Square was formed, of which the "Palais du Parliament" formed one side.

This conflagration, which broke out on the night of 22–23d December, 1719, was caused by a drunken Joiner; it burnt for five days and five nights with great activity. Although most of the houses were at that time built of wood, there seems to have been but one fire engine, and that was old, and out of order. In 1722, they obtained two new "machines" from Holland. Hist. of Rennes, 1845.

had occupied apartments in one of the wings since 1660. The position occupied by his father, as Superintendent of the Finances of the Province, with the anticipation of succeeding to the first Brevet of Farmer-General of the Revenues at Paris, which had been promised to him, seemed to open the most brilliant worldly prospects. "'You were born to live in opulence,' my good mother often said to me,"[5] he remarks in one of his notes.[6] "My earliest recollections," he adds, "are connected with the entertainment given by my father, at his residence in the city, and at his country house of Fricot, in the Faubourg St. Helier, to the Deputies, the Military Officers, and the Nobles, at the time of the meeting of the 'Etats de la Province.' I remember seeing no less than five of our Bishops at his table at one time. We children were placed at a little side table, where our pride, and our love for good things, were alike mortified." "God ordered it otherwise," he goes on to say, alluding to his mo-

[5] "Opulence pour le coup, mais quel danger pour le salut de ses enfans." *MS. Note*, written on the margin of the above memoranda, many years after.

[6] After his birth he was sent into the country to a nurse, according to the general custom of those times. "I remained with my nurse 15 months. She lived at a small village about two leagues from Rennes, on the road to Brest. There were three villages or hamlets, one was called Hell, another Paradise, and the third Purgatory. My nurse lived in "Hell." She sometimes lent me to another poor woman who used to beg, and made use of my presence on one of her arms to excite compassion. This thought has often afforded me pleasure. I always remained much attached to my nurse; her name was Riaedet, and she used to come and see me sometimes, when I was at the Seminary of Rennes in 1808 and 9." *MS. Note.*

ther's words, "my father died (27th February, 1786) a few days after a very painful operation which had been rendered necessary by a fall from his horse—and instead of a succession of opulence, left his affairs in the greatest disorder. Your father, my mother often said to me, could never be made to distrust any one; he believed every person to be good and honest like himself—and the state of his accounts at the time of his death showed it, for not only were all his affairs in confusion, but it was found that he had allowed persons to run in debt to him upwards of a million of francs. The friends of the family, the most eminent lawyers of the city, advised my mother to renounce the succession; but she, very justly, regarded an honourable name as of more importance than wealth, and in order to preserve this to us, she determined to take upon herself the management of his affairs, even at the sacrifice of her own property.[7] She accordingly addressed herself to the task, and with the assistance of two accountants, Messrs. Jourdain and Henaut, for whom she has often charged me to preserve feelings of lively gratitude, she worked day and

7 I find a similar preference of a good name to wealth, in the admirable Memoirs of the Marchioness De La Rochejaquelein:

"I had been destined in infancy to be the wife of the Marquis de Lescure. His father dying in the year 1784, left him 800,000 francs of debt. Although advised by lawyers to renounce the succession of his father, he had the delicacy, as well as the Countess de Lescure, his grandmother (his mother was dead), to become answerable for the whole."—*Memoirs of Marchioness De La Rochejaquelein.*

night until she got my father's accounts in order; and owing to her diligence and management, the losses were much less than they would otherwise have been, and his debts were all paid."

It is evident, not only from the circumstances here related, but from her conduct during the Revolution, her Letters to her son, the manner in which he always alludes to her in his Memoranda and Letters to others,[8] that Madame Bruté was a woman of more than ordinary intelligence and strength of character. This was regulated and directed by a fervent and devoted piety. There can be no doubt that, under God, the eminently religious character of her son, which caused, we may say, every thought, word, and action of his whole life to be guided by Faith, was owing to the instructions and example of his excellent mother.

He was happy also in enjoying, during those tender years, when the character is formed, the guidance of one of the best of Priests, the Abbé Carron,[9] so well known for his labours in England, and

[8] "My mother," he says in one of his memoranda, "was a woman of strong mind (forte tête), understood the world and had great experience in business matters, but always faithful to her Religion, hid the Priests and assisted them in many different ways, during the Revolution; the respect of all classes of people was a great protection to her and her family in the worst of times."

[9] Guy Toussaint Julien Carron, born at Rennes, 1760. Having distinguished himself by his zeal, and particularly by his charity towards the poor, he was imprisoned in 1792, for refusing to take the civic oath. Exiled the same year, he founded several churches and schools in England. Returned to France in 1814. Died in 1821. He was author of a large

the admirable books of piety which were written by him. "My first confessor," he says in 'Some Remembrances, before my first Communion,' "was Mr. Carron, Vicar of the Parish of St. Germain, then a very young Priest, but already so remarkable for his exemplary life, and most fervent piety, that he was called 'The Abbé Térèse,' in allusion to St. Teresa. This was soon after the death of my father, when I was about eight years old. I remember well that the first time I went to confession to him, he gave me, as I withdrew from his confessional, which stood in the Chapel of the Blessed Virgin, a little Book in French, entitled 'The Death of Abel.' As I was retiring, he came out of the Confessional, and gave me the Book. I remember his face, as it appeared at that moment, with such an expression of amiability and piety upon it. I was his penitent for several years, until 1791, the last year of the free exercise of Religion in France, during which

number of works of piety. Bishop Poynder preached a funeral Sermon at the service celebrated for him at London. The celebrated Lamennais, who in his better days lived with him, and revered him as a Saint, had collected materials for a biography of the Abbé Carron, but never wrote it. The Baron D'Eckstein, in an article in the Rambler for May, 1859, on the Abbé de Lamennais, whom he had known intimately, says: "In contrast with Lamennais, I may mention a Priest who had a heart of gold united with a true knowledge of men, the Abbé Carron, the only Priest to whom Lamennais always did justice, and whose death was an irretrievable misfortune for him. This man had the *genius of goodness.*" In a letter to Bp. Flaget from the Mountain, dated June 9, 1821, Mr. Bruté mentions the news of the death of M. Carron at Paris: "my first spiritual Father—so often called the Saint Vincent de Paul of our days."

year I had the happiness of making my first Communion. I went regularly to Confession, but up to that time, thanks be to God, my excellent mother, and I must add excellent teachers, I had little to confess. Although I had attended the public schools for four or five years, I was an entire stranger to all improper notions—and my chief matter of reproach, at the time of making my general Confession for first Communion, was the having taken[10] an apple from the stand of an old Fruit-woman. During the same interval, I learned my Catechism at School, though at times I attended the public Catechism at the Parish Church, to recite portions of the Holy Scripture, which we learned by heart. I remember, that on one occasion, having repeated the History of the Sacrifice of Abraham, I obtained, as a reward, quite a large print of the 'Annunciation' pasted on a board with a margin of gilt paper around it. It hung for long years by the side of my bed, and I can still call to mind the strange, vivid associations of the Blessed Virgin and good Father Carron, in my childish impressions of piety and holiness of life. My first Prayer Book also made a great impression on my mind. It was

[10] I need not say that these notes were written without the least expectation of their ever being seen, except, at any rate, by the eyes of intimate friends. I have taken it upon myself, however, to publish them, not only because they afford a pleasing picture of Bishop Bruté's early life, but also as throwing light upon the state of education and religion in France immediately previous to the Revolution.

a 'Paroissien,' bound in green morocco, with gilt edges, and was given to me on the very day of my father's funeral, February 28, 1786. I had long desired to have one, and I presume there was not a little vanity mixed up with the devotion with which I followed the Mass and Office in my beautiful Prayer Book, at the College and the Parish Church. I had it in my possession twenty years afterwards, with its broken covers, defaced binding, and some torn leaves, but I lost it somehow or other in my many journeyings. I made my first Communion, as I have said, in 1791. There were about 200 of us, of the first or second Communion, for it was the excellent custom of those times to make the second Communion with the same preparation as the first, after a short spiritual retreat. I thank thee, O my God! for the state of innocence and piety I was in the day I performed this most important act."

The place in which this Retreat for first Communion was conducted seems to have been a very strange one. From an allusion to it, in one of his memoranda, I would infer that it was what might be called the Hall of the Charnel-House of the Cemetery near the Church. He speaks of it as "a long narrow room filled with benches, with the skulls and bones of many generations of those who had preceded them, piled, according to the custom of our cemeteries, in a sort of upper story over our heads, so that we could see them through the lattice work which surrounded them. This sight made us very serious and devout, especially on the first day of the Retreat. I do not remember anything in particular in regard to the instructions that were addressed to us, except that they were, as usual, on sin, death, judgment, the divine Sacrament, the happiness of serving God, &c.—and that they made upon us the impressions they were intended to produce. I walked among the tombs during the intervals with some of my companions, and I remember that we were very much in earnest, and animated one another by our remarks, and by our expressions of respect towards the good Priests who conducted our Retreat, especially Mr. Carron and Mr. Desbouillon—this last a saint of goodness, and penance, and zeal, and charity towards the poor, and a heavenly preacher—but a small, ugly, odd looking man, so that some of us burst out into a laugh at a curious comparison which he made,[11] and the strange gesticulation by which it was accompanied. Oh! how sorry we were, and when the instruction was over, we went to him and asked his pardon, which he so kindly and cheerfully gave us. He is dead long since, and I have no doubt a Saint in Heaven. Whilst other particulars have

[11] Bishop Bruté was naturally of a cheerful disposition, and had a strong sense of the ridiculous, as is attested by many little pen and ink sketches amongst his papers; some of them would do honour to Hood or Cruikshank.

vanished, the general impression it made is still strong on my memory. I remember, however, the many sittings by the Confessional of Mr. Carron, in the Chapel of the Blessed Virgin, in our huge Gothic Church of St. Germain; the small Statue of our Blessed Mother, in a white and blue mantle on the altar—and the last evening when I received absolution; the effort to make a good act of contrition, and the earnest desire for a good Communion, a good death, and heaven—and then going to say the 'Miserere' on my knees, on a huge tomb near the High Altar, where we were to receive our Lord the next morning. The events of the next day it would indeed be hard to forget; the early rising—the prayer for the soul of my dear departed father—the benediction asked from my mother on my knees—the spirit of recollection and devotion which I cherished, in view of the important act I was about to perform; somewhat disturbed by the anxiety of our good Mr. Leblanc, in regard to my dress and 'frisure,' and the huge Candle I was to carry. I remember singing the Canticle of Fénelon, 'Mon bien aimé ne paroit pas encore'—the departure for Church—seeing our friends coming from all sides—the entrance of the Church—all seated in rows so near one another, yet such good order and silence—so much fervour in singing the Canticles—such an indescribable suspense and delight of the heart until the moment should come to receive: but before doing so, reciting, in front of all, the act of Consecration, with Térèse Champion for my companion, as the representative of the girls. Twenty years afterwards when I returned to France, I found her, still so faithful in her perseverance, so devoted to our blessed Lord. It seems strange to me now, that all distinct remembrance of the act itself is lost. I am sure it was all Faith, and pure desire of union with God, and of the Thanksgiving afterwards, I only remember the sincerity and ardour of the offerings . . . the return home, with poor Lamirel, the lad put to the charge of my mother, who for many years after that, until he had got his trade, fulfilled towards him that happy duty, imposed that day upon all the young communicants belonging to the more respectable families, of choosing from amongst the poor a 'brother of Communion,' to be taken care of and brought up as a member of the family. My heart is full, when I think of that day—thanks! thanks, O my God."

The above memoranda show how lively were Bishop Bruté's recollections of the events and persons of his youth. His papers afford abundant evidence how closely his heart clung, at all periods of his life, to the memory of his native City and Province. Sometimes it is a little sketch of a building or Church,[12] within the City, or in the suburbs, done with his pen, with a few words of affectionate remembrance, or some circumstance which occurred there, written under it.[13] Sometimes a fuller description, recalling the ancient religious glories of his much loved Brittany and his own recollections of the place and the persons who dwelt on the spot described in his time. It is to be regretted that his memoranda upon these subjects are of so fragmentary a nature—being generally merely hints, or words to assist his memory, rather than detailed descriptions which would now be so interesting. From one of these pages of jottings, as they may be called, it appears that at the time of his father's

[12] The drawing and notes on the opposite page will give an idea of these sketches, of which there are several among the Bishop's papers.

[13] The following notes are written under sketches of the places referred to—

"*St. Cyr*, a Priory before the Revolution, where I used to go sometimes for a walk with my good mother—a military depot from 1792 to 1814—then an asylum for penitents, under Mother Eugénie—said Mass there when I was in France.

"*Paimpont*—the ruins of the Abbey—the woods and ponds—so calm and solitary.

"*La Chapelle Bouexie*—the abode of my sister—the Chateau—the Chapel—the woods—the immense masses of Rocks—a mile beyond, the ancient Chateau de la Harlai, and on the other side, to the right, the still more ancient Chateau de la Roche—the animals feeding in the narrow valley between them—the little shepherds—and above all the chapels—the masses—the good old Priests—and the peasants, 'ces bonnes gens' who used to welcome me to their Cottages, with so much cheerfulness and kindness—all is present to me, and the recollection brings back to my mind the days and feelings of my youth, and the places I shall never see again—O my God, thou art my only good, and the only true life is that which is eternal."

1. The Cathedral—formerly the Abbey Church—St. Melanie, founded by St. Melanie in the 6th century, possessed his reliques, and also those of St. Amand, like him one of the early Bishops of Rennes. I remember seeing the Benedictines there in their habit, and was present several times at the services in 1787-1788. The impression made upon my mind by the majestic simplicity of their ceremonies and the divine chant is still fresh in my mind, and the sound of their voices as they chanted the psalm, "Cum invocarem, &c.," in the office of Complin, still echoes in my ears and in my heart—and then the benediction and the sound of the big bell of the Abbey at that moment. In 1791 the Church and Abbey were usurped by the Revolutionary clergy, in 1792 they became the prison of the Catholic clergy who remained faithful to their vows and would not take the new oath. I visited them twice whilst they were confined there, disguised as a baker's boy and carrying a big bread basket on my head. In 1793-94 the Church was turned into a stable for the cavalry, in 1795 into the City Hospital, that having been taken possession of for an Arsenal, in 1802 restored to divine service as the Cathedral of the Diocese.

2. The Bishop's Residence—a more modern building—the "pavilion" on this side changed into a Picture Gallery, that on the other into a Botanical School in 1799, restored to the Bishop 1802. The Duke of Angoulême lodged there in 1814.

3 The Gardens of the Evêché, and [4] their extension, forming a beautiful Botanical Garden, opening upon the country towards St. Michael and the magnificent prospect of Belle-vue [6], two miles eastward, and towards St. Lawrence [7], three miles.

5. The Garden of the Abbey.

8. The Promenade, called "Thabor," belonging to the Abbey, with its superb terraces, made by the Benedictine Novices during their times of recreation. How often have I walked there alone or with my good Mother, the prospect most extensive, including the Château de Caillé, belonging to the virtuous and charitable house of Montluc-Cicé. I revisited all these beloved spots in 1815. I have made this sketch and written this note during recreation, Evening of Palm Sunday with little hope of ever seeing them again.—Eternity.

death in 1786, he was at a boarding school, kept by Madame Badier, in the Parish of All Saints, which was as he mentions one of the largest Parishes in Rennes—he alludes to the narrow street, opposite the Church, through which they were accustomed to pass, when they took their promenade on Wednesday of each week—the Church itself—the entrance—the high Altar—the "Eternal Father"[14] over it, the Chapel of Mr. Rebulet—the procession of Corpus Christi—the Assumption, with the grand Statue of the Blessed Virgin—of Palm Sunday, &c. He adds, "I note down these remembrances in 1821, on the Feast of All Saints, 34 years after; everything is still fresh in my mind and present to me; I could describe everything—the street—the signs of the shops—the shops themselves—the fruit stalls—the bells on the Vigils of the Feasts—the Glas (the passing-bell for the dead) during the whole evening before the Feast of All Saints." In a memorandum headed "Places where I have studied"—which, from its minute details, seems to have been written as an exercise of local memory, it appears that his first school, where he learned to read, was kept by a certain Mademoiselle Rosé in the "Rue aux Foulons," and that the "Pension" of Madame Badier, above alluded to, was his second

[14] In a note he speaks of a mason who was killed by a fall in 1794, while attempting to pull down the "Eternal Father." The Church was burnt this year (1794), with 40 houses; the ruins were afterwards removed, and the spot left open.

school. With his lively imagination, tenacious memory, and excellent disposition, he must have been an apt scholar from the commencement, and seems to have won the affections alike of his Teachers and fellow students. He attended the College[15] at Rennes from 1788 to 1791, under the

15 The following memoranda are written on the back of a "Sketch of Mr. Sorette going to Class:"

"As usual all the Establishments of Instruction, below, were gratuitous, under the patronage of the Bishop, the parliament, and the mayor and echevins.

"*The College of Rennes.*

"M. FAJEOLE, Principal; retired—
"M. DUBOIS, his successor, died; most worthy priests.
"M. BOURGES DE BLERY, Principal; died as a saint 1805 or 6.
"M. SORETTE, priest; martyr.
"M. MILLAUX, priest; Superior of the Seminary since 1810.
"M. ROSAYS, simple layman or tonsured.
"M. DUFOUR, ditto.
"M. DE CHATEAUGIRON, Priest; died at London, author of many pamphlets. I have his picture.
"M. GERME, Rhetoric; Layman, since rector of the Academy.
"M. LE BRETON, Moral Philosophy; excellent priest, afterwards curate at Chateaubourg, since his return from England.
"M. MAYNER, Natural Philosophy; excellent priest of great talents; After him
"M. CABRYE, died I think in England, also a most worthy priest
"M. DAMON, Vice principal; Priest in England, curate of Erbrée since his return; a modest, holy, and very well informed priest.
"M. DUCHESNE, Academy.
"M. MERIEL, Fencing.

"This college formerly under the charge of the Jesuits; then from 1500 to 2000 Students; much less after their expulsion; yet in my time between 5 or 600 Students; besides a school of Law, one of Medicine. The Seminary for ecclesiastical Students, and another for the candidates, both under the Eudists MM. Morin, Blanchard, Beucher; between 2 or 300 Students together. The school for the young nobility, above 100, under those excellent priests, too, MM. Leforestier, Perdriel, &c.; another school for the young ladies of the nobility—l'Enfant Jesus."

particular supervision of the Rev. Mr. Sorette, of whom he has given so touching an account, in one of the following sketches.

During this year (1791), in which as we have seen he made his first Communion, the Legislative Assembly passed the most severe laws against all the Clergy who refused to take the oath to the "Civil Constitution of the Clergy,"[16] and as almost all refused to do so,[17] the open and public

[16] The Constituent Assembly having (Nov. 4, 1789), confiscated all the Ecclesiastical property, and (March 19, 1790) suppressed all Religious orders and congregations, proceeded (Aug. 24, 1790) in its work of "decatholicising" France, by enacting the famous "Civil Constitution of the Clergy," which virtually abrogated the Catholic Church, in that country, so far as it was in the power of man to do it. By this famous Law, the State assumed to itself the power of conferring ecclesiastical jurisdiction; the Bishops and Parish Priests were to be chosen by the electors, in the same manner as the members of the Assembly; they were forbidden to apply to the Pope for Confirmation, but were permitted to write to him as visible head of the Church in sign of unity. As soon as it became a Law, the most violent measures were taken to oblige the Bishops and Clergy to take the oath to it. Out of 135 Archbishops and Bishops in France four only took it, Loménie de Brienne, Card. Archb. of Sens; Talleyrand-Périgord, Bishop of Autun; de Savines, Bishop of Viviers; and Jarente, Bishop of Orleans; the great majority of the Clergy also refused to take it. Hence the distinction of 'Prêtres sermentés et insermentés' so common at that time. Pius the VI. condemned the Civil Constitution of the Clergy by several briefs, and Monseigneur de Boisgelin, Archbishop of Aix, drew up in opposition to it an "Exposition des principes sur la Constitution Civile du Clergé," which was signed by all the Bishops except the four above mentioned. The Civil Constitution is now remembered only as a specimen of the folly of those days and as a lesson for the future, if men ever learn anything from such lessons, which is very doubtful.

[17] The following Letter, a copy of which, evidently taken at the time, I found among the Bishop's papers, is interesting, as having been written by an eye-witness:

"Letter of the Abbé De Pierre, ocular witness of what occurred at St. Sulpice last Sunday, on the occasion of administering the civic oath.

exercise of Religion may be said to have ceased in France. The College at Rennes was broken up, and from this time Mr. Bruté pursued his studies under private teachers. In the list of " places where

"MONDAY, January 10, 1791.

"You are right, my dear friend, in thinking that the great majority of the Curés of Paris, and especially the Curé of St. Sulpice, would not take the oath. Since the publication of the decree, the emissaries of the Jacobin Club have been constantly going from Curé to Curé endeavouring to persuade them to take it. Mr. Bailly was particularly charged to look after the Curé of St. Sulpice, whose adhesion the Jacobins were especially anxious about, on account of his personal merit, and his great influence over his numerous assistants, and the Clergy of the city in general. But all the philosophy and eloquence of the mayor have failed before the piety and devotion of the Pastor. On Sunday, the day fixed for the presentation of the oath, more than ten thousand persons, two-thirds of them parishioners, and the rest understrappers (gagistes) of the Palais Royale, filled the Church of St. Sulpice. The Curé had been forewarned by more than twenty Letters that they would proceed to the greatest extremities, if he would not take the oath, pure and simple, with all his Clergy. They informed him also of the bloodthirsty declarations which had been made against him and against us in the Clubs and Coffee Houses of Paris. Nevertheless he preached a discourse on Christian Charity, before the High Mass, as usual, and with that force and eloquence which you know so well. As soon as he had finished a thousand voices were raised, demanding him to take the oath, under pain of being dragged out of the pulpit, and hung up to the lamp-post with all the priests belonging to the Church. All sorts of imprecations, menaces, and a frightful tumult on one side, the most calm, but firm and immovable countenance on the other. Already the cohorts of the Palais Royale were pressing forward toward the Pulpit, and the Curé and all the Clergy who surround him would infallibly have become victims of their refusal to take the oath, if it had not been for the prudence and courage of a body of the Grenadiers of the National Guard, who had been placed at the foot of the pulpit, to protect our lives in case of necessity. The sixty *Vicaires*, the Superiors of the four religious communities of St. Sulpice, and all the good Priests residing in the Parish, surrounded the Pulpit during the Prone. As for me, my dear friend, I was at the side of our good Curé, and at the approach of the phalanx I seized him in my arms, and would have carried him in this manner, in the midst of the Clergy and good Soldiers, to the grand Sacristy; but just then, several

I have studied" he put down "four years under Mr. Muriel." During these days of persecution (1791–96) he seems to have remained most of the time at Rennes, in his Mother's residence,[18] but

companies of the National Guard came in by the side doors and restored order about eleven o'c. The High Mass was then commenced. After the 'Pater' the Municipality entered and received the oaths of Messrs. Bonnay and Henoy, hired Chanters of the Church, who, as you well know, form no part of our Community. To put a climax to this imposing ceremony, a Capuchin and six others who had not taken the oath, in cassocks, asked and obtained the privilege of taking it on this occasion. The Curé, the sixty *Vicaires*, the Superiors of the four Seminaries, and the Priests and Chaplains of Communities within the Parish, renewed their profession, and swore before the altars to suffer hunger, persecution, and death itself, rather than take the civic oath, and thus betray Christ and his Holy Church. You will thus perceive, my dear friend, that the Community of the Priests and Clergy of St. Sulpice have remained faithful, and the municipality have been obliged to content themselves with this silly and useless proceeding. The same ceremony will be repeated next Sunday, on account of the eight days' grace, granted by the National Assembly, not without a design, to the Clergy of Paris only; but the Curé and Clergy of St. Sulpice will disappoint them. In fact, we have nothing to fear for that day at any rate. Mr. Dansel, a Doctor of the Sorbonne, whom you know by reputation, and who wrote the 'Apology for the Civic Oath' which created so much rejoicing among the demagogues, on account of the well-known learning and virtue of the author, has retracted, and has written a Letter upon the subject which is making many converts, even in the Clubs —'Confortare et esto robustus.'

Thy friend in life and death.

"DE PIERRE DE BERNIS."

18 I find endorsed on the back of a Letter received by him in 1796, from the Abbé Desprès, the following note: "This Letter is from M. Desprès, before the Revolution Curé at Reguiny, in the Diocese of Vannes, then in prison at Vannes. He had been a long time in concealment at Rennes, in the House of Mr. Trublet, and I studied my philosophy under him." The "Sketches" will show how great an interest he took in those holy confessors who at that time suffered and died with such heroic constancy. Afterwards, when they were confined in prison instead of being immediately condemned to the scaffold, he seized upon every opportunity of visiting them in disguise to carry them the Blessed Sacrament. He

portions of it were spent at La Chapelle Bouexie, where his half-sister Madame Jaussions resided. The Notes, short and imperfect as they are, will convey to the reader some idea of his manner of life during that dreadful period. Amidst all its alarms and sufferings, his memoranda show that he was exact and regular in the employment of his time. He rose early,[19] and no doubt found in

mentions that as a boy he would go and enter into conversation with the guards, so as to become known to them and get opportunities of visiting the prisoners, with Letters for them concealed in his clothes and sometimes the Blessed Sacrament on his bosom, followed by a Priest in disguise.

19 The following Notes, written on a loose sheet of paper, were among Bp. Bruté's MSS.

EARLY RISING.

"To day (26th Ap. 1819) I received a letter from my mother, dated the 2d of January, 1819. She was born in 1736, and is consequently in her 84th year. 'My health is very good,' she writes, 'no pains—sleep soundly,' &c. She used to consider early rising, to which she was always accustomed, a pledge of longevity. 'No longevity, my son,' she would say to me, 'except for those who rise early'—but she regarded it from a higher point of view than the mere enjoyment of health and prolongation of life —at least, in these blessings she saw the instrument of better ones. Early rising, she would say, is absolutely necessary for any one who would faithfully discharge his duties in life; it secures health, gives clearness and soundness to the head—calmness to the mind—freshness to the thoughts and affections—is favorable to pious dispositions—and affords leisure for recollection and meditation, so as to begin the day well, before the hurry of the more advanced hours surrounds us with the labors and distractions of common life. And my good mother was right—there is no indulgence more carefully to be guarded against than that of lying abed in the morning. One hour retrenched by a firm resolution to confine our bedtime to what is necessary, is half a month added to each year of our life; two hours, which many could retrench (and some even more), is a whole month. Six hours of sleep is enough alike for old age and youth (childhood requiring more); according to the apothegm of the Salernian School, seven we grant to the lazy, eight to nobody.

those studies, of which he was always so fond, some relief from the anxieties which in those days of terror must have disturbed the most fearless and best regulated minds. "He acquired in boyhood and youth," says Dr. McCaffrey,[20] "habits of study, of close and patient mental application, which he retained through life. In spite of that modesty which prevented him from ever speaking in his own praise, I could learn from a long and intimate

'Sex horas dormire, sat est juvenique senique,
Nos septem pigrio, nulli concedimus octo.'

Early rising affords to the virtuous soul the most favorable opportunity of exerting her empire over the body—for so great is its fondness for rest and indulgence, so strong an effort does it require to break the pleasing chains of sloth and to give up the easy bed and the quietude of its slumbers, always the more agreeable towards morning when lightest (and to a certain extent conscious), that it requires each morning a true act of fortitude and self-denial to rise at the appointed time. It is almost the only task that habit does not make easier. My mother enforced this duty, which brings so many precious advantages with it, with the anxious firmness of true love.

"When the poor boy of 12 hesitated to jump out of his bed at 4 or 4½ o'c. in summer, or 5 or 5½ in winter, stretching out his arms, rubbing his eyes, and sighing pitifully at the sound of his mother's voice, 'Gabriel! Gabriel! debout'—she would begin in a half gay and half serious manner to sing a verse of one of the good Abbé Carron's canticles:

'N'attendez point cet age
Ou les hommes n'ont plus
Ni force, ni courage
Pour les grandes vertus!'

O my mother! how can I ever sufficiently thank you for all your considerate kindness—ever anxious to form your children to habits of virtue and self-denial."

[20] Discourse, on the Rt. Rev'd Simon Gabriel Bruté, D.D., &c., by the Rev'd John McCaffrey, Prest. of Mt. St. Mary's College, Emmittsburg, 1839.

acquaintance with him, and from the testimony of others, that, in the public schools of his native City, he was distinguished, and eminently successful. His after life proved it. His mind was too rich in treasures of classic lore, too amply furnished from the armories of science, for him to have been a dull or careless student. Whether he conversed with a friend or lectured a class, or heralded the message of salvation from a pulpit, the evidences of profound knowledge as well as of remarkable genius incessantly flashed before you. Whatever he once read, or studied, he remembered. Even in the last years of his life, when his attention seemed to be absorbed in Theology and other branches of ecclesiastical learning, he recited with ease all the Fables of La Fontaine, entire scenes of Racine, Corneille, and the finest passages of the other French writers, or of the Latin Poets. Though less familiar with the Greek classics, he had read them with advantage as well as pleasure, and turned to good account his knowledge of their language, in the study of the Greek Fathers of the Church. At one time he had in view to enter the French Polytechnic School, and for this reason he pursued a very extensive course of Mathematical science. Subsequently he had the best opportunities, in the medical school of Paris, of penetrating deeply into the mysteries of Chemistry and Natural Philosophy. He improved them with his usual diligence. While he devoted himself to severer studies, he gave some share of attention to music and drawing; and in the latter of these accomplishments he attained a proficiency which in after years was a source of pleasure and advantage to himself, and a means, which he often happily employed, for the purpose of interesting and instructing others. His studies were interrupted by the Revolutionary troubles, and he spent about two years in his mother's printing establishment, during which he learned and practiced the business of a compositor. It would appear that he was led to this much less by inclination, than by the reverses which his family had sustained, and the dangers of the times." This admirable sketch of Bishop Bruté's intellectual character and application is fully confirmed by his Note Books and Manuscripts in my possession. I find no allusion amongst them, however, to his having pursued the business of a compositor, although he mentions in different places the various manners in which he was employed, and I am inclined to think that if he ever worked in a printing office it was only for a very short period, as a means of protection during the very worst period of the persecution.[21] He began very early

21 Since writing this, I found on the back of a sheet on which he had written some remarks on the art of Printing, the following note: "In 1793-4, during the height of 'the Terror,' my mother made me work in the

in life to keep a journal, or, as it may more properly be called, a Note Book. The earliest ones are lost, having probably been destroyed by himself for fear that they would be found by the Gendarmes, in some of their domiciliary visits, which were so frequent during those times. The earliest memorânda which I find amongst his papers are upon some loose leaves, which have been evidently torn from a book of this sort.[22] They are dated in 1795,

printing office to save me from being enrolled in a regiment made up of children, named 'The Hope of the Country,' and a hopeful set they were. They requested and obtained permission to take part in the 'fusilades,' which they often did. When the deputation whom they sent to request this permission presented itself before the Revolutionary tribunal, they were requested to take their seat alongside of the judges, and preside at the condemnation of some victims, who were handed over to these young scoundrels to be shot. This regiment was formed of boys, of 14, 15, and 16 years of age. My mother was much pressed to allow me to join them, and was terribly alarmed on this account. I remained in the printing office nearly a year, and became a pretty good compositor."

22 In the few leaves left, the names, except the Capital Letters, have been erased, evidently for the same cause.

The following simple incident exhibits in a striking manner the terror of those days, when a pious Letter from a friend was preserved with fear lest it should serve to criminate alike the writer and the receiver of it. The Abbé Carron wrote a note to him two months after his first communion, from Jourdelais near Rennes, dated 3d July 1791, in which he encourages him to perseverance in the path of virtue, and gives him some excellent advice in regard to his conduct and studies. On the back of it Bp. Bruté has written: "This short note is a monument of the cruel persecution which had then commenced. It was written to me from the country, where this good Priest had taken refuge, having been driven away from our Parish of St. Germain in the city. I have never seen him since. He emigrated to England, and I was almost afraid to keep this memento of him in my possession. I changed his name by inserting a 't,' making it Carton, and erasing the name of his holy friend M. La Gueretrie, of whom he speaks, and whom I have since seen when Superior of the Seminary of Rennes and afterwards Curé of Vitré."

when the storm of violent persecution had somewhat abated. These memoranda are very brief and imperfect, and throw little light upon his own personal history, though they would afford no doubt much that would be interesting to a native of Rennes, or a local Historian of that part of Brittany. Their chief interest to us consists in the manner in which they mark the gradual change of feeling amongst the people, and the reaction against the Revolution on account of the atrocities which had been committed in its name and under its influence. For this reason I have translated many of them, and placed them as an Appendix to this volume.

On the 10th of February, 1796, he began the study of medicine with Mr. Duval, an eminent Surgeon at Rennes. His copious memoranda of subjects studied, operations assisted at and performed, show with what earnestness he pursued them, and how soon he became skilful himself. He makes no allusion to the motives which caused him to choose this profession—but we may not doubt from his whole character, that it was not so much any peculiar attraction which he had for it, as because it would afford him an opportunity of being useful to his fellow creatures. Thoroughly imbued as his heart and soul were with attachment to his Religion, there is no evidence that at this time it had entered into his mind to devote himself to the Ecclesiastical State—or if he did, the continued persecution directed against anything connected with Religion rendered any such aspirations apparently hopeless. His earnest application to his medical studies did not, however, in any manner impair his attachment to his Faith, or his interest in everything and every person connected with it. Amongst his papers are Notes and Letters written to him by Priests, in confinement at Rennes and elsewhere, thanking him for his words and acts of sympathy and kindness.[23]

[23] The following Letters were written to him at this time from the Prison at Vannes by the Abbé Després, previously alluded to as Professor of Philosophy :

"VANNES, 21 Thermidor, year 4.

"To the Citizen Bruté at Rennes.

"Have you, dear Citizen, received my Letter? I sent it to Barré in order that he might forward it to you either by some safe opportunity or by the Post. In our present rigorous imprisonment, it is forbidden us to speak or write to any one. Our keepers tell us that it is contrary to the Law, but we know nothing of any such Law, or the makers of it. I hoped that we might hear, through you, some news of our brethren at Rennes. To-day a rumor reached us that we were to be set at liberty; but we do not know on what foundation it rests, and my object in writing to you at this time is if possible to get some information in regard to the matter. You may be certain that your promptitude in answering me will not equal my impatience to hear from you. When there is a fixed limit to sufferings, they can be endured with patience. The assurance that they will have an end at a certain fixed time mitigates them, but the uncertainty in which we live is most oppressive.

"We expect therefore that you, who are at the source of the news, will let us know upon what foundation the uncertain reports which have reached us are founded. Have the prisoners in Rennes been set at liberty? One thing is certain, that they will be long before we are. The Department of Morbihan is full of zeal in enforcing rigorous laws; they do not wait even for the official announcement of them. But, when the question is of any relaxation of severity, they are very slow in acting upon them.

After having pursued his studies for two years under M. Duval, he went to Paris, in 1799, to continue them in the medical school there. There he of course enjoyed every advantage in the way of instruction. He attended the Lectures of Pinel,

I was myself arrested before the law had been officially promulgated, and others were arrested before I was. Please also let me know of Citizen Trublet; I heard that he was very ill, from some sailors who were brought here by force, having been taken from their homes to serve in the ships of war. You may suppose what sort of blessings they invoked upon the Republic and its agents. Recommend me, my dear friend, to your good mother. I find great consolation in your friendship, which I value highly.

DESPRES.

"Write under cover to Barré. One of our companions named Maner, from Lower Brittany, was taken from this place yesterday, and carried, as we understand, to Rennes. Endeavor to get some information as to his fate, and inform me when you write. A thousand kindnesses to Augustine, and your companions. Do not forget, above all, the Mademoiselles Chat . . . . (Chateaugiron).

Supra.

"To the Citizen Bruté with the Citizeness his Mother, Place of Equality at Rennes."

"To the Citizen Gabriel Bruté at Rennes.

"VANNES, 30 Messidore, the year 4.

"I can assure you, my dear friend, that I have received no greater pleasure, during the eight months of my imprisonment, than that afforded me by your Letter. It was dated the 19th and I received it the 28th. What a happiness to me, to know that neither you, nor your mother, nor your companions, who were so dear to me, have forgotten me. But why did you not say something of the Demoiselles Chateaugiron, and my confrères who are in prison at Rennes—why have you told me nothing about them—are there many of them? Are they all confined in the Tower (the Tour du Bat)? Are any permitted to visit them? Are there any hopes of their being liberated soon? The similarity of our situation makes us anxious to hear about them. There are 24 of us, confined in the small Convent (au petit Couvent), and 3 who are still in the Prison, but who were taken out of the dungeons soon after us. Seven others have perished on the Guillotine, and another has died of the Jail Fever. This is the name they give to a sort of contagious Fever, which formerly was very fatal in

Esquirol, Fourcroy, Bichât, and other eminent Professors, and according to his custom made notes of all that he heard which was likely to be useful.[24] Many of these distinguished men were avowed advocates of the prevailing infidelity, and

the prisons of Vannes. We are lodged in the Garret of the 'Petit Couvent,' without being permitted to hold communication with any one within or without. Some persons have come fifteen or twenty leagues to visit us, but they would not allow them to speak to any one. Barré, however, made out to get in, by some means or other, and, as you may suppose, I was both surprised and delighted to see him. I do not believe that the Chouans have demanded any thing for us ; they have not demanded half enough for themselves. A large number of them were brought here from Cloermel and Josselin, and confined in the Tower, and this morning they were carried to Nantes.

"It seems that those who are in power here had determined on my death, as I have been informed by one in their secrets ; but God did not deem me worthy of the sacrifice. My sickness caused them to hesitate, or rather to delay my death, and for a long time they were uncertain what to do ; and now, they have determined to wait for new explications of the law. So that in reality my sickness, of which I complained, and asked the cure of God, was what saved my life. God knows always what is best for us. My health is still very poor, but better than when I was at Rennes ; tho' I get very little exercise, being permitted to walk about two hours each day in a little narrow court, where the air is very bad. I live on bread alone, having taken a disgust to meat of every sort. Adieu, my good friend—I beg your mother to preserve me a place in her remembrances, and especially in her prayers. I never forget her in mine. Remember me also to the Mademoiselles Chateaugiron, and your young comrades, whom I embrace with the most sincere affection.

"DESPRES, DE REGUINY."

[24] These notes, amounting to several closely written Volumes, are amongst his papers in the possession of Archbishop Hughes.

It is related of him that in one of his journeys on foot to Baltimore, he was obliged to put up at a lonely house, the only spare bed in which was claimed by a Doctor who had preceded him. They entered into conversation upon the subject of medicine, and the Doctor was so much delighted with the pupil of Pinel and Bichât that he insisted upon Father Bruté's taking the bed. *MS. Note by Wm. Miles, Esq.*

took advantage of every occasion to sneer at Religion, and inculcate their false principles. His early religious training, which had preserved his Faith and Morals during all the horrors and privations of the Revolution, stood him in good stead at this time, and rendered him proof against the sophistries and ridicule to which he was now exposed. Not satisfied, however, with practising and openly professing his Religion, he entered into a combination with several of his fellow students, particularly those from his own Province, boldly to oppose the false principles to which they were obliged to listen.[25] They chose such subjects for their Thesis before the class as enabled them to avow their belief in revelation, and to defend its truth. One of the beneficial effects which followed from this course, was that the attention of the

[25] Mr. Bruté was at this time a member of the Society formed by the saintly Abbé Delpuits, ex-Jesuit, who preserved so many youths from the evil principles of the day, and brought back large numbers to a sense of religious duty, by gathering them into a religious congregation or Confraternity, similar to those established by the Society of Jesus. In a Letter to Bp. Flaget, dated April 14th, 1812, from Baltimore, he says: "Mr. Delpuits, our good Father of the Congregation, is dead; pray for him. It is to him I owe my preservation at Paris, my entrance into the Seminary, and consequently my coming here." In the same Letter he mentions having received Letters from France from Mr. Duclaux (Director at St. Sulpice), Mr. De Lamennais at St. Malo, and others, and give details in regard to the closing of the "Petit Séminaire" at Rennes, of the Trappists having been driven away from the "Forêts des Camaldules," and of 60 workmen having been sent at 3 o'c. in the morning to break to pieces the Crucifixes, and destroy the Stations on Mt. Valerien (near Paris) which had been recently restored. He adds: "It is Fouché who has been recalled to the Ministry of Police, who thus signalizes his return to office."

Government was called to the subject. Buonaparte, then First Consul, was labouring to restore Christianity in France, as the necessary means of reorganizing Society; and the infidel Professors were made to confine their teaching to its proper limits.

He graduated at the Medical School in 1803 with the highest honours.[25] There were at that time

[26] An incident occurred whilst he was a Student of Medicine which illustrates his fidelity to his friends, and his earnest fearlessness of character. One of his fellow students, named Collin, had been called upon to attend a person who had been wounded by the explosion of the Infernal Machine (24th Dec. 1800), which had been intended to kill Buonaparte, and neglected to give information to the Police; for this he was arrested and tried, and confined in Prison. Mr. Bruté had in vain made every exertion to obtain his liberation, and finally, when a Student at St. Sulpice and one of the Clerks appointed to serve Mass at the Tuileries, took the bold expedient of presenting a petition in favour of his friend to the Emperor in person. He seized the moment when Buonaparte was leaving the Chapel and ran forward to put the petition in his hand. Buonaparte, absorbed in thought, moved too quickly for him and did not see him—it may be said, luckily—for he ran the risk of being shot dead as an intended assassin. He afterwards succeeded in having his friend's sentence commuted to exile to the Mauritius. The petition to "Buonaparte, Premier Consul," in favour of his friend, written in a clear round hand and signed by himself and Frain, a fellow student from Brittany, is among the Bishop's papers.

From the following memoranda, which I found among his papers, it would seem that a story had gone about that he himself had been implicated in the affair of the Infernal Machine. The report no doubt had arisen from his interference in the case of Collin.

"25th January, 1834. Remarks (pour souvenir a *l'occasion*) by your friend and Chaplain at St. Joseph's.

"1st. I never in any manner belonged to La Vendée—a student at Rennes, for the Polytechnic School, and afterwards of Medicine, I never quitted my native city, until I went to Paris, to the Medical School, in 1799, at twenty years of age.

"2d. At the time this occurred, I was entirely wrapt up in my medical studies and preparing for the prize.

cleven hundred Students attending the course ; out of these one hundred and twenty were chosen by "concursus" as the best—and amongst this number, Mr. Bruté received the first prize, after another examination.[27] He was immediately appointed physician to the 1st Dispensary in Paris, but having already determined to study for the Church, he refused it, and soon afterwards entered the Seminary of St. Sulpice. He was not led to abandon a pro-

"3d. A Physician (Collin) from our country (Brittany) and a fellow student with us at the Medical School, was called to attend one of the Conspirators who had been wounded, and was cast into prison because he had neglected to inform the Police. It might have occurred to any one of us, and we all interested ourselves warmly in endeavouring to obtain his release, regarding him as a victim of a secret of honour and medical duty. As he was from our Brittany, I naturally was very active in his behalf. All the Professors encouraged us in the attempt. After having been kept in prison six months, he was condemned to stay another six months. At this time he was let out on condition that he would exile himself to the Isle of France, and I was accepted as his security. The Prefect at Nantes, through favour, making an excuse of the English blockade, permitted him to remain there. He was still in that city when I, being in the Seminary of St. Sulpice, was appointed the first Clerk in the Imperial Chapel, and made an unsuccessful attempt to petition the Emperor in his favor.

"In 1808, being a Priest and Professor of Theology in the Seminary at Rennes, I never for a single moment had anything to do with any political movements of any sort. I came to this country in 1810, and returned to France twice, in 1815 and 1824, but without having *seen* one of the Bourbons, or received any favours at their hands. I might add also, that as regards M. de Cloriviere, with whom I have been confounded since his death, I had never seen or knew him, until my arrival in this country in 1810, when he was at the Seminary, which he left as a Priest, for Charleston. It was by Letters and by personal intercourse at the 'Visitation,' after his return, that we became friends. In 1824, when I visited France, I made the acquaintance of his respectable and religious family."

27 He sent the reward to Mr. Duval, his Teacher at Rennes, as a mark of gratitude. *See Journal.*

fession to which he had devoted so many years of assiduous study, and which opened its most brilliant prospects before him, as Dr. McCaffrey remarks, "from any feelings of disgust. He always honored it, as one of the noblest to which a highly gifted and philanthropic man can devote himself. Delightful as his conversation was to all, and to men of science in particular, it was peculiarly so to the student, or to the practitioner and professor of medicine.[28] They often expressed their astonishment, that after a lapse of twenty or thirty years, engrossed by the pursuits of a very different order, he retained so perfect and minute a knowledge of all that he had studied in his youth, under the great masters of the French capital." He turned from it only because he had higher and more important objects in view. His eleven hundred class-mates in medicine told him that it was easy to find Physicians for the body, but the Revolution had made it more difficult to find Physicians for the souls of men. For ten years, the Houses of Religious Education and Seminaries had been shut up. The Guillotine and Prisons and privations of exile had spared but a comparatively small number of the former Clergy, and of these many were occu-

[28] He was never known, however, to practise it, after he became a Priest, except on one occasion many years after, at Mt. St. Mary's, when one of the pupils having broken his arm, and the Physician not being at hand, he set it for him, "most skilfully," as the Doctor said when he came. *MS. Note*, *Wm. Miles*, *Esq.*

pied in foreign missions. Dreadful as had been the ravages of infidelity and impiety, and the almost entire privation of all spiritual succor, an immense number of the French people still remained faithful to their religion, and a new supply of Levites, to fill the places of those who had perished, was called for on every side. One of the first matters to which the new Bishops turned their attention was the re-establishment of Diocesan Seminaries, in order to provide for these pressing wants. These were the circumstances, no doubt, which influenced Mr. Bruté to seek admission into the Sanctuary. Such a determination could surprise no one who knew him. His whole life, even in the world, had already been a preparation for it. At a different time it would probably have been his first choice—and having chosen it now, he gave himself wholly to the work. He always studied with his pen in hand, and his manuscripts again mark the exactness and extent of his new studies. Theology was a science for which his mind was admirably fitted. He loved his Religion, and it evidently became his delight thoroughly to explore the very foundations of it. In Note-books made at this time each subject is developed and illustrated, as if his place had been that of a Teacher, instead of a Scholar.[29] Bp. Bruté was never a surface student,

[29] One of his resolutions at a Retreat in 1806 is "ne laisser passer

but now he became emphatically a foundation one. The works of the Fathers of the Church, the acts and canons of her Councils, as marking her tradition, were carefully studied by him. From this time until the end of his life everything that he read or studied was with this view. His voluminous memoranda show how carefully he recorded everything which might serve to defend, or illustrate the truth, or to expose and confute error. He made the principles of the various sects his careful study, after he came to this country, and could have written a philosophical history of them, if he had seen fit. No one ever made a more faithful and exact use of every moment of his time. He never was idle, and, as a consequence of this industry, his tenacious memory enabled him to bring forth from the treasure-house of his mind things new and old. To assist him in pursuing these studies, he began at this time to collect a library,[30] which became afterwards a large and valuable one, and this may be said to have been the only property he ever owned. Bibliography was also one of his favorite studies, for he understood not only

aucune matière sans me former un resultat précis de sa doctrine et de sa pratique."

30 Even amongst all the agitations of the Revolution, his Note-book contains memoranda of books mingled with the details of persons shot or imprisoned. When he came to this country and began in the newspapers to defend the Church against the attacks of her enemies, he often regretted the want of works which were needed for the proper exposition of the matter in dispute.

how important a part of knowledge it was to know where learning was to be found, but fully appreciated the value of editions to an accurate student. Although he never wasted a moment over useless books, yet in one sense nothing came amiss to him.[31] He may be said to have been in a good sense of the word a *Heluo librorum.*

It is not necessary to say, that to one animated by such dispositions, and so well prepared to make a good use of every opportunity, the four years he spent in the Seminary of St. Sulpice were what the Scripture calls "full years." He advanced alike in solid piety and sound learning. Having completed the usual course, he was, after having passed through the intermediate steps,[32] ordained Priest, in the Parish Church of St. Sulpice by Monseigneur André, the retired Bishop of Quimper, on the Saturday before Trinity Sunday, 1808.

The Bishop of Nantes was very anxious to

[31] "They say that it is an ill mason that refuseth any stone; and there is no knowledge but in skilful hands serves either positively as it is, or else to illustrate some other knowledge."—*Herbert.*

[32] He received the Tonsure on the 22d of December, 1804, from Monsig. De Belmont, Bishop of St. Flour, acting for the Card. Du Belloy, the Archbishop of Paris; Minor Orders 21st December, 1805, from Monsig. De la Roche, Bp. of Versailles; Sub-Diaconate 31st May, 1806, from Monsig. Du Voisin, Bp. of Nantes; Diaconate from Monsig. Enock, Bp. of Rennes. M. Emery was at that time Sup. of the Seminary, Boyer, Duclaux, Garnier, &c., Directors. Among his fellow-students were Monsigs. Fayette, afterwards Bishop of Orleans; Du Bonald, the present Card. Archb. of Lyons; Mazenod, the present Bp. of Marseilles; Forbin-Janson, the late Bp. of Nancy, &c.

obtain his services for his Diocese, but the Bishop of Rennes, who knew his value not only as an instructor, but as a model for the young Levites of his Diocese, appointed him Professor of Theology in the Diocesan Seminary. His own spirit of zeal and devotedness seems even at this period to have turned his mind towards the foreign missions. It is evident from the notes of his Retreat,[33] that he had already arrived at a great spirit of detachment from home and family (and no one ever loved them more dearly) and was prepared to make all the necessary sacrifices, the moment that he felt it to be the will of God that he should leave France. Those who knew him in after times will not be surprised to learn that in the list of sacrifices to be made, if he goes on the foreign missions, that of not being able to carry his Library[34] with him occupies a prominent place. At this time (1807) he

[33] M. L'Abbé Duclaux, of whom he often speaks with the greatest veneration, "mon saint et tout bon père," was his director. In Sept. 1806, he made a Retreat at the *Carmes*, to ascertain his vocation in this matter; again in 1807 his views were towards India. According to his usual custom, the pro's and con's are all written down. I find many notes amongst his papers in regard to the different foreign missions—the way of getting to them, &c. He made a plan of going on *foot* to India, founded upon some statements for sending troops to Syria. It seems to have afforded him much pleasure to think that his medical studies would prove useful to him on the Eastern missions. In his Retreat of 1807, he appears to have determined to go, so far as rested with himself, under the particular protection, as he adds, "of the Blessed Virgin, in her Immaculate Conception."—*Idées de la Chine.*

[34] "Se priver d'approfondir mes études de lire les SS. Pères,—ma Bibliothèque."

appears to have determined to go, and I cannot ascertain from his memoranda what induced him to remain. It was probably the authority of the Bishop of Rennes. He had already refused his services to the Bishop of Nantes, and no doubt felt that they were needed at his new Seminary. In consequence, after his ordination he proceeded to his native city, and entered upon his duties as a Professor of Theology. The Bishop at the same time offered him a Canonicate in his Cathedral, which dignity he however refused.[35] Although he no doubt discharged with zeal and fidelity his new and important duties, and made use of the opportunity to continue the studies of which he was so fond, yet it is probable he never abandoned his resolution of devoting himself to the missionary life. If he did, a circumstance which happened the following year again renewed it. The Rev. Mr. Flaget, of the Society of St. Sulpice, who had already been several years (1792–1808) on the mission in the United States, was nominated in 1808 to the new See of Bardstown in Kentucky. Anxious to escape the proferred dignity, he went to France in the autumn of 1809, in the hope of being permitted to decline it, but on presenting himself to M. Emery, the Superior of St. Sulpice, he found

[35] Dr. McCaffrey states that he was also offered the position of assistant chaplain to the Emperor. The offer of the Canonicate is from a manuscript note in his own handwriting.

that the Sovereign Pontiff had given an express order that he should accept the office to which he had been called. In consequence, after having remained in France a few months to obtain fellow-labourers for his extensive but uncultivated Diocese, he returned to the United States in 1810, and was consecrated by Archbishop Carroll on the 4th of November of that year. It was no doubt his presence in France that renewed in Mr. Bruté's mind the intention of devoting himself to the foreign missions, and turned his mind towards the United States. Having obtained his Bishop's consent, he sailed from Bordeaux[36] in company with the Bishop elect of Bardstown, in 1810, and arrived in Baltimore on the 10th of August of that year. For nearly two years after his arrival he was retained as Professor of Philosophy in the Seminary at Baltimore. In 1812, he was sent for a few

[36] I find on a slip of paper amongst his manuscripts a note of the name of the vessel and a list of his fellow-passengers. She was a brig or barque, named the George Dyer, Capt. Peter Collard. There were several French and American gentlemen—amongst the Americans a Dr. Johnson, bearer of despatches from Gen. Armstrong, at that time our minister at Paris, "*a Poet*, an Ursuline nun; five Trappists, the Père Mauvais and four brothers; one Jesuit, Father Cary; Mr. Flaget; a relative of his, Mr. Gras; Romant, Derigand, Deidier, Chabrat, Bruté."

Father Bruté always retained the greatest love and veneration for the venerable Bp. Flaget. He often wrote long Letters to him, informing him of the news from France, and of their old companions and friends in their always beloved country, De La Mennais, Fayette, good Father Garnier, Boyer, &c. His Letters to Bp. Flaget also contain many interesting particulars in regard to the history of the Church in this country.

months on the mission at St. Joseph's,[37] on the Eastern Shore of Maryland, where he received the Letter directing him to go to Mt. St. Mary's College, near Emmittsburg,[38] "to aid Mr. Dubois,"

[37] Among his Letters to Bishop Flaget, I find the following note, which was probably one of his first attempts to write in English: "Day of St. Frances of Chantal, Baltimore, being there these two days—Je suis exilé sur l'Eastern Shore of Maryland, where I serve with Mr. Monally, at St. Joseph's, Talbot Co. I went there the first days of vacation. I am trying to learn practically my English. I have said Mass and preached, bad preaching as it may be, in six different places. This must force this dreadful English into my backward head, or I must renounce forever to know it. I have seen Mr. Marechal only a moment; he is gone with the Archbishop (Carroll) to Carroll Manor. He will come back on Monday, but on Monday I will be making English and blunders on my Eastern Shore."

In another Letter he gives a laughable account of his attempts in English, and of Father Vincent's (the Trappists' Superior) *bold essays* in preaching. One of his manuscript Discourses, however, unhappily got disarranged, and he found himself deep in the peroration, instead of the exordium, before he discovered his mistake.

[38] Emmittsburg would form an admirable subject for a local History, connected with the origin and progress of the Catholic Religion in Maryland. The old log Chapel at the Elder Station was put up before the Revolution. The village dates back to 1788. The Church in the village was built in 1793-4. The Mountain Church 1805-6. The Elder House stood for many years surrounded by the primeval forests. It was the place of worship for many years of the Catholics in that part of the country, the Elders, Brawners, Livers, and others of English descent. It was an influx of Irish Catholics which caused the Church in the village to be built. When Mass was first said at the Elder's Station the Priest came from the lower part of St. Mary's Co. The first Priest at the village was the Rev. Matthew Ryan.—*Miles's MS. Notes.*

The Rev. Mr. Dubois assembled the people upon the site of the Mountain Church Nov. 19, 1805; with his usual energy he marked out the spot; the first tree was felled by him that day. They had a barbecue on the occasion.—*MS. Note.*

In 1818, the Sulpicians had the intention of suppressing Mt. St. Mary's and selling the property. The citizens of Emmittsburg made very generous offers to the Rev. Mr. Dubois in order to obviate any such necesas he expresses it. In 1806 the Sulpicians had established a preparatory Seminary at Pigeon Hill,[39] near Abbotstown, Pa., which was transferred in 1809 to Emmittsburg in Maryland, the Rev. Mr. Dubois, who had charge of the mission in that vicinity having already commenced a school there, which afterwards became so well known as Mt. St. Mary's College. It was at first intended to be merely a preparatory Seminary for Ecclesiastical

sity. The Rev. Mr. Bruté in one of his notes says: "15th June, 1818, Mr. Radford came to see Mr. Dubois and told him if he was embarrassed in money matters, the inhabitants of Emmittsburg would supply them. Mr. McMeal, Grover and Boyle, offered $1,500. 28th. In the evening Mr. McNeal came to say that they would let him have 7000 or 8000 dollars without int. as long as he wanted it; that if it was intended to sell the Property they would purchase it and give it back to Mr. Dubois. 1st July. A Letter came by Liven from the Archb. which leaves everything in *statu quo.*" The property was transferred at the time, I believe, to Rev. Mr. Dubois.

[39] Pigeon Hill was a Farm or Country seat which belonged to a pious layman, Mr. Harent of Lyon. The Trappists occupied it for a short time. In 1806, he permitted the Sulpicians of Baltimore to commence a "Petit Seminaire" there. It was opened by Mr. Nagot 15th August, 1806, with eight boys. In 1809, Mr. Nagot's health becoming impaired and Mr. Dubois having joined the Sulpicians, the students from Pigeon Hill were transferred to Mount St. Mary's after Easter, 26th and 28th April. Mr. Harent himself became a Priest and a Sulpician at the age of 55; he lived, however, but a few years and died in 1818, in the West Indies, where he had gone on business connected with the College at Baltimore. There were eight students transferred from Pigeon Hill to the Mountain—Columkill O'Conway, John O'Connor, Taliafero O'Connor, James Shorb, James Clements, John Fitzgerald, John Lilly, Jonathan Walker. The Rev. Mr. Shenfelder of Conewaga was the only one who became a Priest from Pigeon Hill so far as I can find; he was a good Priest—died in 1824. The first commencement of Mt. St. Mary's was made by Mr. Dubois in 1807; in 1824 it was detached from St. Sulpice; the Church was built in 1808. The first stone College was built in 1824; when scarcely finished and not yet occupied, it was burnt; the new building was erected in 1824-5.

students, but the great advantages it offered for education induced many parents to seek admission for their sons, though not intended for the ecclesiastical state. The Rev. Mr. Dubois was President of the College, Pastor of Emmittsburg and Superior of the new institution of the Sisters of Charity, which had been lately founded at St. Joseph's under the charge of Mother Seton. These varied duties made it necessary that he should have another Priest with him. The Rev. Mr. Duhamel had relieved him of the charge of the Congregation of Emmittsburg since 1810, but the flourishing condition of the College required additional help, and in consequence the Rev. Mr. Bruté was sent to the Mountain for that purpose. This favoured spot became from this time, until he was transferred to the Bishopric of Vincennes, with the exception of the interval 1815-18, the theatre of his zeal and holy influence—where all the advantages of his most amiable character, his extensive and profound learning, and eminent Christian and priestly virtues, were exerted with the most beneficial effects. He could never have hoped to have done as much good amongst the inhabitants of India and China, by the exertion of the highest apostolic zeal, as he was permitted to do in this country. It is in no disparagement of those holy and eminent men who have adorned the annals of the Catholic Church in this country—of a Carroll, a Cheverus, a Dubois and a Flaget, to say that no one has ever exerted a more beneficial influence in favor of the Catholic Religion than Bp. Bruté. If Mt. St. Mary's, in addition to all the other benefits it has bestowed upon Catholicity in this country, has been in a remarkable degree the nursery of an intelligent, active, zealous Priesthood, exactly such as were needed to supply the peculiar wants of the Church in this country, every one at all acquainted with the history of that institution will allow that the true ecclesiastical spirit was stamped upon it by Bp. Bruté. His humility, piety and learning made him a model of the Christian Priest, and the impression his virtues made upon both ecclesiastical and lay students surpassed all oral instruction. The Catholic Religion alone can produce such men, and hence their example confirms the Faith and elevates the Character of all who come in contact with them.[40] The name of Bishop Bruté has been, and ever will be, associated with that of Bishop Dubois, as common benefactors to the infant Church in this country.

The Sisters of Charity in this country also owe a debt of gratitude to him. Mother Seton found in him an enlightened director and friend; and his advice and influence was most beneficial to her

40 I have often heard old students at the Mountain say, that when they served Bp. Bruté's mass they were overawed by the quiet, subdued, but enrapt fervour with which he said it; at the moment of consecration, in particular, he seemed to be carried entirely out of himself.

young community at St. Joseph's. They were both chosen souls upon whom God had bestowed his most precious graces, and strengthened one another like St. Benedict and St. Scholastica by their conferences on spiritual matters. If she revered him as emphatically a man of God, he regarded her as one who, to use his own language, "if placed in circumstances similar to those of St. Theresa, or St. Frances de Chantal, would have been equally remarkable in the scale of sanctity, for it seems to me," he adds, "that there could not be a greater elevation, purity, and love for God, for heaven, and for supernatural and eternal things, than were to be found in her."[41]

The Rev. Mr. Bruté remained at the Mountain, assisting Mr. Dubois in his various labours in the College, on the Mission, and at the Sisterhood, until 1815,[42] when he visited France for a short time with

[41] Rev. Dr. White's Life of Mother Seton. At her death she left him her Bible, upon the margin of which she had written many notes, which he often quoted and referred to in his classes of Theology and Holy Scriptures.

[42] I find on a strip of paper in his handwriting the following memorandum:

"Landed in U. S. 10th August, 1810. Consecration of three Bishops, Egan, Cheverus, Flaget. I taught Philosophy, preached in French. I visited Mt. St. Mary's and the Valley, July, 1811. Went during the vacations to Pigeon Hill, attended Trappists at the Point 1811. Mr. Marechal arrived; M. Miguel was sent on mission to Eastern Shore in Aug. 1812; Mr. Tuite, Mr. Monally: Went to aid Mr. Dubois end of September, 1812: Went to Frederick to meet Archb. Carroll in Oct.: At the Mountain I taught Latin, French, Natural Philosophy, and gave a Retreat there and at the Sisters'; had charge of the Congregation. Delany died Oct.

the permission of his Superior, to bring over his Library, and to interest the Clergy and people in favour of the missions. He returned in November of the same year, and was appointed President of Saint Mary's College at Baltimore, where he remained until 1818, when, on the death of Mr. Duhamel, he again returned to Emmittsburg and resumed his labours at the College and amongst the Catholics in the vicinity. Mt. St. Mary's College was now thoroughly organized. The Students of the Theological School connected with it acted as Prefects, and assisted as Teachers in the Institution. The system thus adopted by Bishop Dubois is liable to some objections; it interferes, no doubt, with that exact ecclesiastical training which is justly considered of so much importance. Still

1813: Heard of invasion of France coming from the Sisters, 1814: American War, went to Frederick after the defeat of Bladensburg: Went to France with William Seton in April, 1815: Returned in Nov. President of Baltimore (St. Mary's Coll.); do. 1816, do. 1817. Professed Moral Philosophy, Geometry and Natural Philosophy: Journey to Emmittsburg, 1818. Went to Annapolis in Jan. 1818; succeeded in stopping the projected street by the College. Returned to Emmittsburg Feb. 1818, to assist Mr. Dubois after the death of Mr. Duhamel. Was at the Sisterhood until 1822. Took charge of Emmittsburg Cong. until return to France with Mr. Purcell, 1824. M. Wiseman, Emmittsburg. Returned Nov. 1824. Separated from St. Sulpice. Teaching Philosophy and Theology since 1820."

In 1812, at the time of the attack upon Baltimore, Father Bruté had charge of the Mountain Church, and many of his flock went to assist in the defence of the city. He made an address to them on leaving, and became himself so anxious that he walked to Baltimore to join them, and render them such assistance as they might require whilst in the trenches.—*MS. Note by William Miles, Esq.*

even independent of its economical character, it has many advantages, especially for those who are to exercise the holy ministry in a new country, where churches have to be built, and every thing formed. The discipline of teaching and governing boys creates habits most useful under the peculiar difficulties to which a Priest is exposed in a country like this. Under such a system, however, it is of the greatest importance that the Superior of the Seminary should be much more than a mere Professor of Theology. He should be one fitted to keep before those under his charge the living image of a faithful Priest, and capable of forming them to such habits of ecclesiastical virtue as would protect them against the distracting influences of their present duties, as well as the more worldly influences to which they will be exposed in after life. Such a Superior in the true sense of the word was Father Bruté.[43] He understood fully all the responsibility which rested upon him, and never did any one, in his situation, discharge it more faithfully.

A copy of some of his memoranda at this time

[43] The Rev. Dr. McCaffrey has related with the enthusiasm of an admiring pupil and attached friend the many virtues exhibited by Bp. Bruté at the Mountain as a Professor of Theology and missionary Priest. I am tempted to enrich these pages with extracts from this elegant discourse, but it has been happily republished in the "Mountain Memorial," and I would refer all who have not read it and the Discourse on Bp. Dubois (two of the most beautifully written and interesting discourses of this character in the English language) to that work.

will give a better idea of his life than any mere generalities.[44]

The following is headed "One day of a Priest," Eternity.[45]

"4½ o'C. "Benedicamus Domino"—"Praise be to God," on awakening; Vocal Prayer; Meditation before the Tabernacle. Rev. Mr. Hickey's Mass; Jesus Christ my Lord present.

"6 o'C. Celebrated Mass; Jesus Christ present; Breakfast; bodily care. Returned to the Church (on the Mountain), opened the Tabernacle, and took out the Blessed Sacrament. Went with Guy Elder through the woods, our Blessed Lord on my breast. Said our Beads with acts of devotion to the Blessed Sacrament at the end of each Decade.

"8 o'C. At Mrs. McCormick's; her lively marks of Faith and joy; heard her Confession; arranged the table; called the people; the young convert and her little one; her husband preparing for his first communion; administered the Blessed Sacrament to Mrs. McC.; spoke of Martha and Mary and Lazarus and Zaccheus, old friends of our Lord on earth; He still upon earth and we his present

[44] He was fond of drawing out these details on paper, as a sort of help to self-examination. Sometimes notes of what he had taught, of what he had read during the day; how many times he had seen or touched the Blessed Sacrament, &c.

[45] This must have been the first time he was at the Mountain, 1812–15. The word "Eternity" is written upon all his notes and loose papers. The thought of it seems to have been always present to his mind, and to have animated him to fidelity in all his duties.

living friends. On our way to Emmittsburg recited the Miserere, our Father, Hail Mary; Hymn, 'Jesus, lover of my Soul.'

"9½ o'C. At the Church in Emmittsburg; opened the Tabernacle and Ciborium. Went to see Mr. ——, 10 years without making his Easter communion; good *moral* character, as they say; heard his confession: strong Faith, gave lively evidences of it; had a talk with him, &c.

"10¾ o'C. Coming back, baptized the child of Peters' wife; her abundant tears; her great difficulties; did not hear her confession at that time.

"11 o'C. Returned to Church in Emmittsburg; restored B. S. to the Ciborium; stopped at Joseph's with Guy; paid a visit to the B. Sacrament; saw Mrs. Brawner.

"12 o'C. Found at the College an old German woman waiting for me; no duty for ten years; sick and lame; looked very poorly; came to know if I would hear her; Sister Angela gave her a dinner; to come again on Sunday.

"1½. Was called to see Glacken above Emmittsburg; went to the Church at Emmittsburg to get the Blessed Sacrament; this is the fifth time to-day that I have touched my Sovereign Lord, 'The King of Glory,' as Mr. Duhamel has it embroidered on the inside door of the Tabernacle; carried it to the sick; administered the Sacrament of Extreme

Unction; made a little address to those present—several Protestants.

"4 o'C. Went to Mrs. Brawner's; heard her confession; recited my office; Oh! the wonders of that office of the Blessed Sacrament; and am now writing down these notes; but a thousand details, thoughts, and acts not told; how wonderful the day of a Priest. In the Evng. Instructions for Confirmation."

On the same paper is written: "What have I done to-day for the house? Reviewed the 2d Latin Class; had a conversation before God with one of the young men; Latin Lesson; Reviewed the 3d French Class; Latin Lesson to Guy Elder; had a conversation with another young man who came to consult me; one with Mr. Hickey; one with the two Gardiners; wrote a Letter; the Dialogue for Baltimore, six pages; Spiritual Reading, the usual Prayers. If all done well, what a blessing it would bring; but oh! my Lord, so poorly, by halves—alas!"

On one sheet of paper he has written an account of the manner in which he spent the 3rd Sunday in Advent, at the Seminary in Paris, in 1804, when a student there; the 3rd Sunday in Advent at Rennes in 1809, as Professor of Theology; and the 3rd Sunday in Advent, 1819, at the Mountain; the Sundays at Paris and Rennes are the usual exact routine of Seminary Life in France; the Sunday at Emmittsburg is as follows:

"Slept at the Mountain.

"5 o'C. Rose; 1st Prayers.

"5½. On my way to the Sisters (at St. Joseph's), meditation 'en route.'

"6 o'C. Heard confessions; wrote out my meditation.

"7 o'C. Mass. Read De Blois' Lives of the Saints.

"8 o'C. Breakfast at Mr. Grover's.

"8¼ o'C. Gave communion at the Ch. at Emmittsburg to two persons; heard confessions; wrote a meditation.

"10½ o'C. Went to visit Mrs. Hughes and Mrs. Bradley, who are sick; said my 'Little Hours' on the way.

"11½ o'C. Stopped at the Sisters'; read the Life of Madame de Chantal; wrote an Exhortation for the Funeral of Mrs. Lindsay.

"1 o'C. Gave benediction; read the Epistle for the Sunday, and gave a short instruction.

"1½ o'C. Returned to the Mountain. Visited the Sisters at their House [i.e., the Sisters who lived at the Mountain and at that time had charge of the domestic arrangements, Infirmary, &c.]; a few words.

"2 o'C. Went to Mr. Elder's; officiated at Mrs. Lindsay's Funeral; Exhortation. Read the

Hist. of the Councils [i.e., whilst walking, according to his custom].

"3 o'C. Vespers; gave benediction; heard confessions after Vespers.

"4 o'C. In my Room; heard confessions there; Office; looked over some Gazettes 1816–17 [French newspapers]; read in the Encyclopedia account of Pennsylvania.

"7 o'C. Supper; Study.

"8¾ o'C. Evening Prayers; reading, &c." [46]

On another paper, headed "A day of the missions at Emmittsburg"—a holyday at the College, I suppose—he writes down the details of a day's work, spent in going from one family to another, through the country, not visits of friendship or pleasure, but to persons evidently who neglected their duty. He has marked the distances on the margin, and they sum up 30 miles. He left the Mountain at 4¾ o'C. in the morning, celebrated Mass at 5½ o'C. at the Sisters at St. Joseph's, and was home at the College at 6½ in the Evening.

[46] Amongst his papers I find a little slip upon which the following is written in Mr. Bruté's handwriting, and which may serve as an appendix to the above:

"Mr. Dubois, Sunday. His invariable meditation. Then confessions in the Church on the Mountain; Mass at 8 o'C.; again confessions in the Church till 11 o'C.; at 11 High Mass by Mr. Bruté; Mr. Dubois there, at the Sermon. Thus six hours spent in that cold Church. Dinner; we talked. 3 o'C. Benediction, then confessions one hour and a half. At 6 o'C. Catechism of the higher Class (Mr. Hickey the younger one) three-quarters of an hour. Supper at half-past seven. Class in Latin, Jamison, George Elder, Alex. Elder, Grim, one hour; and so on for his Holydays."

He sums the day's work by the following memorandum: "I *remember* to have spoken to 62 persons, more probably in regard to matters connected with Religion and their duty; made a short exhortation at Mass, it being St. Ignatius's Day. Three persons were warned about their Easter duty; several spoken to for circulating evil reports; others warned against attending a camp-meeting to begin next week at Hoover's." On another day he writes: "Saturday night, 14th, I received from Baltimore a number of the *Edinburgh Review*, and Stuart against the Eternal Generation of Jesus Christ. Sunday, 15th. Already read through Stuart's Book, and wrote a long Letter of remarks upon it to Rev. Mr. Elder. Attended to the duties of the day at Emmittsburg. In the evening, read, part on the road, part at home, most of the *Edinburgh*. Monday. This day I finished the *Edinburgh*, made a dozen long notes on the article on O'Meara's Journal, and two on the Article upon Duprat's works, with some search amongst my books in regard to points in these memoranda. Wrote a Letter to Mr. Chanche; packed up the whole to be sent to Baltimore to-morrow morning by Sister Xavier, who is going there. Finished a map of the Ecclesiastical States for the Geography Class. Read on the 6th chap. of St. John, Witasse, Tournely, Drouin, Bellarmine, and the Discussion Amicale; consulted also Wesley's

Notes, Cajetan, Beil, Bergier, my old notes of Mr. Frayssinous, and noted down twenty-one arguments upon the subject. Taught the Class in Theology; studied some other questions; taught the Class in Philosophy; went to a sick call, &c., &c., &c., and then the usual happy round of a Priest, Prayer, Meditation, Mass, Breviary, Beads, visit to the Blessed Sacrament, &c." The following memorandum was made on the 20th March, 1821: "On the evening of the 14th of March Mr. Damphoux arrived at the Mountain to recall Mr. Hickey to Baltimore. The next morning, after I had celebrated Mass at the St. Joseph's, I started on foot for Baltimore, without saying a word to anybody, to speak to the Archbishop and Mr. Tessier, and endeavour to retain him. Stopt at Taneytown at Father Zochi's, and got something to eat. At Winchester found out that I had not a penny in my pocket and was obliged to get my dinner on credit. Arrived at Baltimore (52 miles) 10 minutes before 10 o'C. Mr. Hickey to remain at the College. Laus Deo. Set out on my return the next day (16th) in the afternoon; stopt at Mr. Williamson's, 6½ miles from the city, where the storm obliged me to take refuge. On Saturday, 17th (St. Patrick's Day), said Mass, and made a discourse to the people on the text, 'filii sanctorum sumus.' At 7 o'C. started again, the wind and rain in my face, sometimes so severe as almost to take away my breath; arrived at the Mountain at 10½ o'C. at night. In going I read 388 pages in Anquetil's History of France, the reigns of Louis XII. and Francis I.; 14 pages of Cicero de Officiis; 3 chapters in the New Testament; my office; recited the Chapelet three times. On my journey back, the wind blew so hard that I could only read a Pamphlet of 25 pages (Documents of the Bishop of Philadelphia) and my office." During the time that he was thus busily employed in the duties of his station, and training up so many future Bishops and Priests, he interested himself in anything that could conduce to the refutation of error and the progress of Religion. He contributed constantly to the Catholic newspapers original articles, and often furnished materials for others to use.[47] He carried on a correspondence not only with friends in France,[48]

[47] He took a great interest in the History of the Catholic Church in this country, and made a large number of notes upon it. During his short Episcopate he found time to collect many Historical Notes in regard to Vincennes and the Western country, and communicated several papers to the local journals upon the subject.

[48] Among Bishop Bruté's papers are a large number of Letters from the unhappy Felicité De La Mennais (he came to the Seminary at Rennes when Bruté was Professor there in 1809); they are full of interesting details, and written with his usual facility and beauty of style, apparently full of zeal for Religion, but at the same time overflowing with a querulous, fault-finding spirit, so indicative of self-love and prophetic of his own spiritual shipwreck. He was much attached to good Father Carron, and being obliged to leave France in 1815, on account of his work, "De l'Institution des Evêques," he joined him in London. In one of his Letters to Bp. Bruté, dated "chez M. Carron, Kensington Gore No. 21, Ap. 25th, 1815," he says "John (his brother) collected the matter and I wrote the work, which has displeased equally the Jansenists, Richeristes, and Blanchidistes,

his family and others, but with many distinguished persons in the United States. He assisted Mr. Duponceau in his works on the Indian Languages. He was a friend and correspondent of Charles Carroll of Carrollton, of the distinguished Judge Gaston of North Carolina, and many others.

When the present Archbishop of Baltimore (the

who have been but too powerful in France since the Restoration. But truth has so much force in itself, that it must triumph, sooner or later, over all the vain opinions of men." He adds, "I often think of you; it is one of my great consolations, though, perhaps, we will never meet again until we meet in eternity." In 1816, September 16th, John De La Mennais, the brother, writes from St. Brieux, "Feli remains always with our dear M. Carron. He is at work on an Essay 'Sur l'Indifference en matière de Religion,' which is calculated to make a great impression. We regret (meaning Felicité and himself) that we cannot have your advice and assistance in our undertakings, which nothing can supply." Felicité himself writes to Bp. Bruté from Paris, February 22, 1818: "The 1st vol. (of the Essay on Indifference) has been published, and I have directed Teysseyre to send you three copies. The whole first edition has been sold. No Journal has spoken of it, except the 'Ami de la Religion.' I am preparing a second Edition, in which by the advice of some of my friends (though others oppose it) I will change many things. I will send you some copies as soon as it is out, and if you persevere in your intention of translating it, you had better follow this new Edition. The second volume will be more important; in this I will develop a new system of defending Christianity against Infidels and Heretics." In the same Letter he complains that their old friend M. Carron had not been appointed to a Bishoprick, but "he is not of noble blood, and he remained a Catholic whilst in England" (il est resté Catholique en Angleterre). We have remained always together," he adds; "since we were together in London, we have not left one another. He is a Saint; his zeal and charity are incredible. Pray for me; no one has more need of prayer than I have. Adieu, my dear friend. A Dieu seul.

"F. DE LA MENNAIS."

In some notes of his visit to France in 1824, Mr. Bruté, speaking of De La Mennais and of his Book, says: "Many writings against his 2d volume—some for." "I found," he adds, "all St. Sulpice against it, especially Mr. St. Felix, Mr. Carriere, and Mr. Garnier, &c."

Most Rev. F. P. Kenrick) was appointed coadjutor to the aged Bishop of Philadelphia (Dr. Conwell) and Administrator of the Diocese in 1830, and set himself to work to repair the injuries which had been done to Christian piety and Church discipline by that unworthy Priest, the Rev. William Hogan and his followers—a task for which his virtues and learning eminently qualified him—the Rev. Mr. Bruté interested himself, with his usual zeal, in the good works which were undertaken for this purpose, especially the holding of regular Diocesan Synods and the establishment of a Diocesan Seminary. The great object of his solicitude always was the formation of an intelligent, zealous Clergy, well grounded in the knowledge of Theology and Holy Scriptures, and able to cope with the peculiar difficulties which stand in the way of Catholics, and the Catholic Religion, in this country. In furtherance of these views, he warmly approved of Bishop Kenrick's design to prepare a course of Theology, adapted to the wants of the Catholic Clergy in the United States, where error alike in doctrine and morals presents itself under so many new and startling forms. His numerous Letters to Bishop Kenrick upon these subjects not only give evidence of his zeal and piety, and of his high appreciation of the priestly character, but afford specimens of his profound knowledge of Theology and admirable critical skill. He was no mere bookworm, but had great freshness and independence of thought. It might have been supposed that the scenes he had passed through and witnessed in early life would have made him somewhat of an ultra-conservative—one opposed to all change—but it was not so. Though no one could have been more firm than he was in resisting any attempt to alter or modify anything essential to the true character and office of the Church, yet no one understood better the advantages of judicious accommodation to times and circumstances.

When the Bishops in the United States began to hold Provincial Councils, Father Bruté was appealed to from every side, and his advice was constantly asked in regard to those matters which it was their object to arrange. He had from the time of his arrival in this country been anxious that the Bishops of the country should assemble in this manner, feeling, as he did, how important it was for the progress and stability of Religion, not only that they should meet and confer together, but that proper and uniform rules of discipline should be established throughout the country, while it still formed one Ecclesiastical Province. Many of the beneficial effects which followed the Provincial Councils of Baltimore may be attributed to him.

It was thus, that although apparently hidden in his Mountain retreat, engaged in his quiet duties as a Professor and Missionary, his influence extended on every side, and the whole country may be said, in some sense, to have been the field of his labour. No opportunity of doing good escaped his vigilant zeal. If he heard of a rich Catholic who did not make good use of his riches—of one who was luke-warm in the Faith—of a Priest who was a cause of scandal, or had apostatized, he immediately made use of every influence in his power to bring them to a sense of their duty. By fervent and touching Letters addressed to themselves, and by interesting those who were acquainted with them, he endeavoured to infuse into their souls some portion of the spirit of Faith and Devotion which burned in his own.

His excellent mother died in 1823,[49] and in 1824 he visited his native country to arrange matters connected with her property. His Memoranda show that, as usual, every thought of his heart and every moment of his time was occupied with the interest of Religion.[50] His visits and conversations

[49] She died 28th of May, 1823; he did not receive the news of her death until the 6th of November following.

[50] He took advantage of this visit to make a long Retreat at the Solitude at Issy, under Mr. Mollevaux. I have in my possession the notes of this and of all his Retreats, which he made with great regularity and exactness. They contain abundant evidence of his progress in solid piety and the most intimate union with God. In dwelling during this retreat at Issy upon the particular graces and benefits which God had bestowed upon him, he mentions the holy Priests who had been his spiritual directors at different periods of his life. "Oh! what an account will I have to give," he writes, "of such eminent graces:

"My youth at Rennes—M. Carron.

were all directed either to the spiritual good of the persons visited, or the benefit of the Missions, which he had so much at heart. He returned in the autumn, and immediately re-entered upon his duties at Mt. St. Mary's.

In 1832, when the Cholera had commenced its ravages with so much violence in Canada, and its immediate extension to the United States was anticipated, he wrote to the Most Reverend Archbishop of Baltimore (Whitfield), offering his services when it should reach that city. In August, the Rev. Father Deluol visited Mt. St. Mary's, and the pestilence having broken out in Baltimore, the Rev. Mr. Bruté returned with him in order to attend upon the sick. Immediately after his arrival, he had a violent attack of intermittent fever, and was obliged to return to the Mountain; but as soon as he had recovered, he set off again, without saying a

"During the times of the persecution, so many confessors, martyrs—M. Touchet, M. Sorette.

"At Paris, when a student of medicine—M. Delpuits.

"My Seminary at Paris—M. Emery and M. Duclaux.

"The Seminary at Rennes—A saint, M. Gueretrie.

"The Seminary at Baltimore—Mr. Nagot and Mr. Tessier.

"Mt. St. Mary's—Mr. Dubois. My present Retreat, in the solitude at Issy—M. Mollevaux."

His memoranda made during his visit to Paris and his native place contain many interesting details of his intercourse with Mgr. Cheverus, then Bishop of Montauban, whom he met at Paris; the Count de Senft, former ambassador of Saxony to the French Court; the Baron de Haller; the Card. Prince de Croy, Grand Almoner; the brothers La Mennais, and the celebrated Lannec, his former fellow-student in medicine; M. Daru, and others.

word to any one, for Baltimore, and labored in the Cholera Hospitals there until his services were no longer needed.

One of the subjects, as connected with the progress and solid establishment of Religion in this country, which constantly occupied Father Bruté's thoughts, and upon which he often dwelt in his Letters to Bishop Flaget and others, was the necessity of multiplying Episcopal Sees as fast as they were needed and fit subjects could be found to fill them. He was destined, in the order of God's providence, to co-operate in the work, not only by his advice and exhortations, but by his active exertions. The Fathers of the 2d Provincial Council of Baltimore, in 1833, requested the Sovereign Pontiff (Greg. XVI.) to erect the town of Vincennes in Indiana into a Bishoprick, having jurisdiction over the State of Indiana and a part of Illinois, and the Rev. Mr. Bruté was, on their recommendation, appointed to be its first Bishop. When the news reached him, his humility, and strong sense of accountability, caused him at first to shrink from the burthen which was about to be placed upon his shoulders.[61]

[61] At the time he received the Bulls (May, 1834), he was giving a Retreat to the Sisters at St. Joseph's. He first opened the documents in the chapel on his knees. The next day he went to Baltimore and made a Retreat in the Seminary, to decide whether he should accept or refuse. Every possible consideration on either side is drawn out with the acuteness of a practised lawyer, and the greatest simplicity and fidelity, in his usual detailed memoranda.

With all his zeal and activity, he was very diffident of his fitness for the office, and in one of his written examinations, in which according to his usual custom he states with great simplicity the two sides of the case, he makes out, according to his own view of the matter, a very formidable list of defects; but when he found that the matter was settled, he went to work, not only with the zeal of a good Priest, but the vivacity and energy of a true Frenchman. His only real defect was his imperfect English pronunciation. He may be said to have had every other qualification—natural talent—industrious and methodical habits—great erudition—a high sense of duty—a great spirit of self-sacrifice, and all directed by a will and energy of character which nothing could dishearten or overcome. I have been told that when the matter of his nomination to the new See was debated in the Council, Bishop England was opposed to it, thinking that on account of his love of Books and Study he would not be fitted for the office of a missionary Bishop in the backwoods; but with Bishop Bruté *duty* was the first point, and Bishop England, and every one else who witnessed his short career as a Bishop, must have been surprised at the energy and self-devotion which he manifested. In administrative talent in particular, a great point in a new country, where everything has to be created as it were, he surprised those who knew him best.

As soon as he had accepted the Bulls, he made the necessary arrangements for his consecration, and prepared to set out for the new and arduous field of labours to which the few remaining years of his life were to be devoted.[52]

I find among his manuscripts Notes of a Letter apparently written to the Leopoldine Association of Vienna, in return for some assistance it had given him, and which relates many interesting circumstances connected with his taking possession of his diocese, and his first labours there. Whether it has ever been published, I do not know: "Mere words," he writes, "will poorly express the gratitude of the Bishop of Vincennes for the offering of love and zeal which your benevolent Association has been pleased, in the name of God, to bestow upon his newly created Diocese. The merits of the gift are secure for Heaven for the pious benefactor —may I have my share in them, by making a faithful use of what has been thus committed to my stewardship! It is perhaps proper that, in return, I should give you some information in regard to the beginnings of the Diocese which has been the object of your bounty.

[52] It must have been a great trial to him to leave Mount St. Mary's. It is evident from his Letters that he tore himself away from it with great reluctance. It had bound itself around his warm French heart with the sympathies of a second home. Bishop Bruté had what the phrenologists call the bump of *Locality* strongly developed ; or rather, like all persons of an ardent, affectionate nature, he formed strong local attachments.

"When I arrived in Baltimore from France in 1810, to devote myself to the missions in this country, there was but one Bishop for the whole United States, the late Most Rev. John Carroll. Since then many other Sees have been erected—the See of Detroit, erected in 1833, was the twelfth. The See of Vincennes, erected in 1834, by the Holy See, at the recommendation of the 2d Provincial Council of Baltimore, may be regarded as the 13th. To this see, thus established, I was named as the first Bishop. At the time of my appointment I was and had been for many years Superior and Professor of Theology in the Seminary, connected with the College, of Mt. St. Mary's, near Emmittsburg, in Maryland. Although a large number of Priests now on the mission in the United States had been sent out from this Seminary, at the time of my appointment they were not able to aid me, either with Priests or money. The Sisters of Charity at St. Joseph's, the Mother House, made me a present of two hundred dollars to assist me in establishing myself in Vincennes. On my way to Bardstown, where I was to make my Retreat previous to my consecration, I visited my respected friend Dr. Purcell, the Bishop of Cincinnati, whose diocese must always continue to be a most worthy object of your generosity, as having a large population of German Catholics. He kindly accompanied me as far as Louisville and then returned, whilst I proceeded on my way to Bardstown, where I once more had the happiness of meeting my Father and Friend, the venerable Bishop Flaget, the Patriarch of these Western Missions, upon which he has laboured above 43 years—twenty-five of which as Bishop of Bardstown, having jurisdiction over the whole Western country. I was also permitted once more to embrace my old friend Bishop David, who, having resigned the Coadjutorship of Bardstown, has been succeeded by Bishop Chabrat.

"At the time of my arrival Bishop Flaget was about leaving for Cincinnati, to consecrate the large German Church which had been lately erected. I spent a few days in visiting the different institutions of the Diocese, the College and Seminary at Bardstown, the beautiful Institution of the Sisters of Charity of Nazareth, founded by Bp. David, the House of the Sisters of Loretto, founded by the Rev. Mr. Nerinckx, both having several Academies and Schools under their care. I visited also the flourishing College of the Jesuits (St. Mary's), and regretted very much that my time would not allow of my going to the Dominican Convent and Novitiate of St. Rose. By the time I had finished my Retreat (from 4th to 12th Oct.) under Bishop David, Bishop Flaget had returned from Cincinnati, and I set out with him for Louisville, where Bishop Purcell joined us. Crossing the Ohio, we proceeded directly towards St. Louis, across the vast prairies of Illinois, and passing through the town of Vincennes,[53] half incognito. It was a source of great happiness and consolation to me to pass so many days in the company of these holy Bishops, and to meet that most excellent Prelate, Dr. Rosati of St. Louis. On the 26th of October, assisted by Bishops Flaget and Purcell, he consecrated his new and beautiful Cathedral, which was an occasion of great joy to the whole city. A large body of the militia, and even the United States Troops, from the Barracks near St. Louis, assisted at the Ceremony. Two days after, on the 28th of October, the day of the Holy Apostles St. Simon (my patron) and St. Jude, I was consecrated in the same Cathedral, by the Rt. Rev. Bishop Flaget, assisted by Bishop Rosati and Bishop Purcell. The Sermon for the occasion was preached by the Rev. Mr. Hitzelberger. On the Festival of All Saints, at the request of Bishop Rosati, I officiated pontifically, for the first time. During these days, which was a time of general festivity, there were sermons each morning and evening,

53 In a cheerful Letter to Bishop David from "Salem, half way between Vincennes and St. Louis," he gives a detailed account of this journey, which in itself was no slight undertaking in those days. Once they were caught in a violent storm upon the prairies and suffered severely from wet and cold. He draws as usual a lively picture of their mishaps and adventures, of Bishop Flaget, "l'incomparable," as he calls him, drying his Breviary before the inn fire, &c. They spent only an hour and a half at Vincennes, as he says, without the guns firing or the bells ringing, or a grand procession or anything.

preached by the Bishops or some of the Jesuit Fathers, who have a large and flourishing College at this place, at present our farthest western point, a thousand miles distant from New York, but with another thousand miles of territory extending beyond it to the Pacific, the only frontier of these vast United States.

"Having left St. Louis with Bishops Flaget and Purcell, the Rev. Messrs. Abel and Hitzelberger and Father Petit, we arrived at Vincennes the 5th of November. Some miles before reaching the city, we were met by a number of the citizens, Catholics and Protestants, on horseback, who had accompanied the Pastor, the Rev. Mr. Lalumière, a native of the State, and the first Priest ordained (by Bp. Flaget) for Vincennes. He was of course filled with joy in seeing a Bishop granted to his Indiana, and all the inhabitants seemed to share in it.

"The ceremony of the Installation took place the same evening. Bishop Flaget, who 43 years before had been the missionary Priest here, when it was a simple trading and military Post, in the midst of the surrounding wilderness, proceeded to address the people with his usual fervour. Venerated and loved by all, himself in the 74th year of his age, he introduced to them their new Bishop, no longer young, being in his 54th year, and urged them to make a good use of the privileges which God in his mercy had bestowed upon them. Other instructions were given during these days. On Sunday I officiated pontifically, and on Monday my venerable Colleagues took their leave, amidst the blessings of the whole population, to return to their respective Dioceses. They literally left me alone. Father Petit was obliged soon to return to his College in Kentucky. Mr. Lalumière took charge of the missions in the vicinity of Vincennes, but still 25 or 30 miles distant, and in the whole Diocese there were but two other Priests, one Mr. Ferneding, in charge of the German missions 150 miles distant, and Mr. St. Cyr, whom Bishop Rosati had permitted to assist me for one year, and who was stationed at Chicago, 225 miles off.

"The Cathedral Church, a plain brick building 115 feet long and 60 broad, consisting of the four walls and the roof, unplastered and not even whitewashed—no Sanctuary—not even a place for preserving the Vestments and Sacred Vessels. Only a simple Altar of Wood with a neatly gilded Tabernacle, and a Cross and six beautiful Candlesticks, a gift from France, which were much in contrast with the poverty and utter destitution of the place. The House built for the Missionary, and now the Episcopal Residence, consists of a small, comfortable room and closet, 25 feet by 12, without however a cellar under, or a garret above ; a small plot for a Garden lies between it and the Church, on the other side of which is the Catholic Cemetery. Some years since, the town had a common burying-ground prepared, beyond its limits, and insisted for a while that the Catholics should bury their dead in it like the rest; but they resisted so resolutely they were at last permitted to bury in their own Cemetery. An old wooden building, a short distance from the *Palace*, is occupied by the Servant, and near it is a stable ready for the Bishop's Horse, when he is able to get one. The people are mostly of French descent, poor, illiterate, but of that open, lively disposition which bespeaks their origin. They retain their Faith, love their Priest, but are negligent in attending to their religious duties. They are very remiss also in teaching their children their Prayers and the Catechism, and this causes them to forget it themselves. Many also are in the habit of using profane language. It is true, and should be mentioned, that of late years they have been much neglected, and much of their former piety seems now to be rekindling in their hearts.

"The kind reception I met with on my arrival was followed up by generous gifts of provisions and other necessary things. Of money they have little, and consequently can give but little. A subscription list which was handed around some months after I came, with the intention of providing a yearly income for my support, did not reach two hundred dollars, and most of this was to be paid in grain, if they had not the money at the time. It may seem somewhat out of place for me to enter into such details, but they are necessary to show that although a parish Priest, accustomed to the simplicity of seminary life, may find a sufficient support, yet the resources of the Diocese are entirely inadequate to provide for its great and urgent wants, the education of young men intended for the Priesthood, and building up of those institutions of charity for orphans and others without which Religion can never be firmly established. The Revenue from Pews[54] in my Cathedral is so small as barely to supply what is necessary for the Altar and current Expenses of the Church itself. Of some Property which belongs to the Diocese, but which at present brings no income, I will have occasion to speak hereafter.

"As the Directors of your Association very properly request minute details, in order to be able to form an accurate opinion, I will proceed to give an account of the first six or eight months of my administration.

"A few days after the Bishops who so kindly accompanied me to Vincennes had left, I went with the Rev. Mr. Lalumière to visit his two missions, or Congregations as they are generally named ii.

[54] In a letter to Bishop Kenrick, dated December 18, 1834, he incidentally mentions that the Pew Rent in his Cathedral amounted to the enormous sum of $100, and that the subscription for the support of the Pastor was $240; but not all of this paid. Still there is not a sign of complaint; his only demand, after all, is for Priests. "I am resigned," he says, "to remain at Vincennes alone and attend the sick calls and do all the work myself—but my great, my greatest want is Priests for other places."

this country—first to St. Peter's and then to St. Mary's. The last was not quite completed, and I was requested to name it. It was a great happiness to me to put the first Church, which I was called upon to bless in my new Diocese, under the patronage of the blessed Mother of God; so I named it Saint Mary's, and promised to return again in two weeks and bless it, when it was finished. On the day appointed, all the good people assembled with their worthy Pastor, Mr. Lalumière, at the little Chapel. It was built of Logs, as almost all the buildings still are in this part of the Country. It is only about from 15 to 20 years since these settlements were made. There are about 150 Catholic families, most of them from Kentucky, but some from Ireland. We formed a Procession and went around the Chapel, and the ceremonies were observed as closely as possible; then I celebrated Mass and gave an Instruction to those who were present. Some Baptisms and a Marriage filled up the labours of the day, marked as the first on which I blessed a Church in the wilderness. The conduct of the people was full of edification.

"Afterwards I visited some of the places around Vincennes, where I found small clusters of Catholic families. At the Cat's River, 13 miles from the town, I had more than 25 or 30 families to attend, and every time I went there I saw how much more gcod would be done by a resident pastor. I will soon send one to them, though for the first few years he will have to be supported chiefly from the means at the Bishop's disposal. Once they are firmly rooted, however, such missions will support themselves. The people are mostly of French origin. I visited another Congregation in Edgar County, on the Illinois side of the Diocese, about 70 miles from Vincennes. It is an American Settlement from Kentucky, with some Irish families among them. There are perhaps 50 or 60 families within a circuit of 15 miles, and I found them as at St. Mary's truly zealous for their religion, and talking of the Church which they would soon build, and the Priest that would soon be sent to them.

"At Vincennes I undertook to bring our long neglected youths to their first Communion. At Christmas I had twenty, some of whom I had prepared myself as well as I could. Others I put off, intending to prepare them during Lent. Sixty more made their first Communion at Easter, many of them 17, 18, and 20 years old. The following Sunday I administered the Sacrament of Confirmation for the first time in the Cathedral of St. Francis Xavier to about 90, mostly the same who had just made their first Communion. I say nothing of the difficulty of the task, as it would look as if I were commending exertions, the poor results of which I have rather to lament before God. I simply mention what may give the Association a proper idea of the task of the Bishop, and of the situation of the newly erected Diocese.

"Having a population of about 1,500 souls under my immediate pastoral care, every Sunday I had to give two instructions, one in French, and one in English, and then to administer the Sacraments. In the eight months I had 65 Baptisms, 10 Marriages, and 20 Burials, and a great many sick calls to attend, often six, seven, and ten miles from home. Then there were a number of other visits to be made, poor to be seen to, Protestants to instruct, &c. I received four men into the Church, two of them upon their death-bed

"Much of my time was also taken up by the extensive correspondence which devolved upon me as soon as I was sent to Vincennes, and also by the numerous communications I continued writing, as I had long been in the habit of doing, for the religious papers, particularly the *Catholic Telegraph* of Cincinnati. That kind of work is continually called for by our position in this country, and the influence exerted by it too important to allow it to be neglected. Over the signature of 'Vincennes' a series of letters were published, in which the ancient labours of the Society of Jesus in this region, from the Lakes to the Mississippi, were described. Our very town took its name from a

French officer, M. De Vincennes, who was massacred an age ago by the Indians, together with a Jesuit Father who had accompanied him in an expedition to protect the friendly tribes who lived upon the Wabash, where the Society had established the mission of St. Francis Xavier. Others of these Communications consisted of a sketch of the country and its aborigines, an account of the former difficulties which religion had had to contend with, her obscure and precarious beginning, her present hopes, the inducements offered now to Catholic settlers, and also the steps taken by the last Council to obtain the erection of the new Diocese, comprising Indiana and a part of Illinois. They were followed by an account of our present transactions, and a pastoral Letter which I had given after my Consecration, and which had been published in the newspapers of Vincennes and in all our Catholic journals. In that Letter the Protestants themselves were affectionately addressed, and the intentions of the American Bishops and our Holy Father at Rome were explained in such a plain and simple way that left no room for the absurd charge of their being influenced by political and not simply by religious considerations, and that no foreign conspiracy or danger for the civil institutions of America was involved in this new carrying out of the original Divine Commission given to the Church by her Lord: 'Go and teach all nations.'

"Being convinced of the fact that we could not obtain missionaries from the other Dioceses, I determined to try to obtain some from abroad. Before setting out, however, for this purpose, I wished to examine myself the west and north of the Diocese, while Mr. Lalumière would go through the south and east and make a report of his observations to me, so that I could start without much delay on the journey in which I am now engaged. After Easter, in company with an honest and pious man of Vincennes, I went through Illinois, visiting again Edgar County for the Paschal duty, and then proceeding north as far as Chicago on Lake Michigan. Mr. St. Cyr had arrived there from St. Louis and enabled the Catholics to make their Easter Communions, so I gave only a few Confirmations, and three instructions, one on Saturday and two on Sunday, to encourage the rising Catholic Congregation of that most important point. It is now composed of about 400 souls of all countries, French, Canadians, Americans, Irish, and a good number of Germans. The Garrison of the Fort, the Commandant, and part of the Staff and band of musicians attended. In general, it may be said that the military are always friendly to the Catholics and their services, which they are free to attend if they choose.

"From Chicago we went round the end of Lake Michigan to the River St. Joseph and the mission of the Rev. Mr. De Seille at the Indian Village of Pokegan, situated just outside our Diocese, and in that of Detroit. This mission was established many years ago by the venerable Mr. Badin. Mr. De Seille has lived for three or four years at Pokegan's Village. He has there and in the neighbourhood more than 650 Catholic Indians baptized. A large number of their huts are built around the Chapel, which is constructed of bark with a Cross erected behind and rising above it, and filled with rudely made benches. The Indians begin and end their work without hammer, saw, or nails; the axe being their only implement, and bits of skin or bark serving to fasten the pieces together. The room of the missionary is over the Chapel, the floor of the one forming the ceiling of the other. A ladder in the corner leads to it, and his furniture consists, as did the prophet's, of a table and chair, and a bed, or rather a hammock swung on ropes. Around the room are his books, and the trunks which contain the articles used in the Chapel, as well as his own apparel. He spends his life with his good people, sharing their corn and meat, with water for his drink, and tea made from the herbs of his little garden. He abjures all spirits, as all the Catholic Indians are forbidden to touch that which is the bane of their race, and he would encourage them by his example. I attended at the evening Catechism, Prayers, and Canticles, and in the morning said Mass, at which a large number assisted. Through the Interpreter I addressed a few words to them.

"On Thursday evening we arrived at South Bend, a little town beautifully situated on the high banks of the St. Joseph River. It is growing rapidly, owing to its many advantages. Crossing the river we visited 'St. Mary of the Lake,' the mission house of the excellent Mr. Badin, who has lately removed to Cincinnati. He had a school there kept by two Sisters, who have also gone away, leaving the place vacant. The 625 acres of land attached to it, and the small lake named St. Mary's, make it a most desirable spot, and one soon I hope to be occupied by some prosperous institution. Rev. Mr. Badin has transferred it to the Bishop on the condition of his assuming the debts, a trifling consideration compared with the importance of the place.

"On Friday morning we left for the Tippecanoe River and the village of Chickakos. The Indians had heard of our coming, and had sent some of their number in advance to ascertain our movements. They gave notice of our approach to others who had camped out a few miles to wait for the Bishop, and make a more worthy escort for him. The Chief Chickakos was there and directed their movements. Coffee had been prepared at a small village only three miles from the principal one. We dismounted, and sitting on mats of woven straw partook of their kind cheer. Then we crossed the river, and soon arrived. On our way Mr. De Seille pointed to a poor mother sitting on the bank with an infant child lying in her lap who had been recently baptized, and was now near death. He told me that it would be a great consolation to her if I would give her my blessing, and tell her of the happiness awaiting her little angel. I did so, and could see by her silent and resigned expression that she felt comforted.

"Chickakos' Village is not so large as Pokegan, yet the Chapel is nearly as large. It is however without ceiling, and without a room for the missionary overhead. The mission being of later standing, Mr. De Seille had baptized only about 120 persons, of whom I confirmed 16. He was to remain there two weeks, to prepare many more for baptism and some for their first Communion. He said he found some difficulty in preparing the Indians for their first Communion on account of his not being sufficiently master of their language to make use of the proper terms in treating of the Holy Eucharist. He begins to understand it now, yet when he speaks to them he prefers to do so through his interpreter, a Canadian woman born of an Indian mother, a truly excellent and deserving person. She is 70 years of age, and yet preserves a strength and activity truly wonderful. She followed us on horseback, and was very ready to assist us. On our arrival all assembled at the Chapel, and Mr. De Seille introduced me to them as their Bishop, the head in these parts of all the other 'Robes Noires' (Black Robes), the name which they have given to the Catholic Priests, or Jesuits, for it is all one to them. He added that I had no one above me, on earth, but the Great 'Robe Noire' beyond the high seas, the chief of all the Christians in the world, meaning the Pope. He said that every 'Robe Noire' that would come to them must come as sent by the Bishop, and then be received; otherwise they should have nothing to do with them. The Chief Chickakos said a few words in reply to show that they were well pleased, and promising that they would meet together the next morning to give a more special expression to their feelings. Accordingly, on the Sunday morning, having informed us that they were ready, Mr. De Seille and myself sat upon two little stools in the Chapel, and some twelve of the leading men came in and took their seats upon some of the opposite benches. Chickakos made the speech, and I was very much struck with the concluding sentence of it, when, raising his eyes and his arm towards Heaven, and then pointing to the ground—having previously expressed their confidence in Father De Seille and in me, and their readiness to receive me as their Bishop, and their desire to show it by presenting me with half a section, 320 acres, of their land—he said that 'God, when He would return from Heaven to visit our Earth, would see that ground, to which he pointed, which they were giving me, and that it would prove to Him their sincere devotion to His holy religion and the messengers he had sent to secure its blessings to them.' To this I replied through the good interpreter. We then made our preparations for Mass and the administration of the Sacrament of Confirmation. Before Mass six children were baptized by me. My instruction was on prayer, and the gifts of the Holy Ghost. Mr. De Seille told me that he had observed in them all such a deep sense of the eminent privilege of prayer, and the dispositions it required, as are not found, as often as they should be, among the best instructed Christians of more favored countries. I saw most unequivocal evidence of it in their behaviour in the Chapel, and the affecting, earnest way in which they listened to the instructions, repeated their prayers, and sang their hymns, and I was very much edified. Of the 16 that I confirmed, one was an old Chief, who since his baptism had led such an innocent life that he had not been observed to commit any fault, or give way to impatience, or any other imperfection.

"We slept on the benches of the Chapel, and some of the straw from the floor, wrapped up in our great-coats, after the manner of the good Father. Our food was boiled corn, fish, venison, and wild turkey, minced together in one dish, and some cranberries broken and mixed with sugar they get from trees. Our drink was water. Coffee was not to be had, although this was the principal village.

"In the afternoon Vespers was sung in Ottawa, and, as I should have mentioned before, by the aid of printed books. Many used them, as they are very quick in learning to read, and have retentive memories. Some knew the whole contents of their prayer-books. They contain all the usual daily prayers, and exercises for Confession and Communion, a pretty long Catechism, and a large number of Canticles, with many of the principal Hymns and Anthems of the Church. Among others, they have the 'Pange Lingua' and the Psalms for Vespers translated in Ottawa.

"I was to leave them after Vespers, so, before we began, they came to sign the deed of the land presented to the Church, which we had drawn up in as legal a form as we could, putting the indispensable condition that the act was subject to the approval of their temporal Father at Washington, as they call the President of the United States. Although many know how to read, none know how to write, so Chickakos and some of his friends made their marks on the paper, and two Canadian traders who were present signed their names as witnesses. It remains now to be ratified by the President.

"After a few parting words, and giving them my blessing, we mounted our horses, and were escorted for some miles by a large number, Chickakos at their head, who before leaving us dismounted from their horses, and asked their Bishop's blessing again. Mr. De Seille was to remain two weeks there giving instructions, and preparing the Indians for Baptism and First Communion. Some time after, I received in Vincennes two long Letters from that excellent Missionary, giving me a most interesting account of the exercises of the two weeks which he had spent there, at the end of which he had baptized 80, and admitted 30 to their First Communion. He said that the coming of a Bishop, 'a chief man of the true prayer,' as they called him, and head of the 'Robes Noires,' had excited much joy among all the Indians. They remembered when the Jesuits left the country, after the conquest of Canada by the English, how their Fathers had hoped until their death for their return, and, dying without that consolation, most earnestly recommended to their Children to be looking for them when they should come, and to receive them and believe them to be the true messengers of God. We spent the night at the house of a settler 15 miles from Chickakos, and found the house so full that many had to lie on the floor, as I had done once on my way to the Lake. Here we had a bed for two, as was often the case. Through all that journey of 600 miles, we seldom came to any regular taverns, but almost every family would allow you to share their meals, and give you a place under their roof, receiving on your departure a small compensation, which however is sufficient to remunerate them. Our old friend, for one evening's acquaintance establishes that relation between us, told me in the morning, when I asked for the bill, that he used to take nothing; but as he could not well stand that, and wished still to help any stranger, he only took what strictly sufficed. He was of the sect called 'Christians.' After supper he had said to us, 'Friends, I ought not to interrupt our family rule on your account; we are about to have our Evening Devotions. You can remain with us, or if you prefer to retire I will show you your room.' We thanked him, and said that we would rather retire. This did not displease him at all, or prevent him from bestowing every attention upon us. We were almost always thrown upon the hospitality of Protestants, and were treated kindly by all. I improved in every family such opportunities of conversation as were afforded me, and passed such simple remarks as would make them acquainted with our Faith and practices, and remove some of the prejudices which they had acquired from their parents or the ministers of the places from which they had come to settle in the West. They listened to what I had to say, and as very few ministers have as yet come to these remote parts, I found that it would be easy to preoccupy the ground. But, alas! we have not the means to do so, nor Priests enough to send to the dispersed sheep of the house of Israel, to the domestics of the Faith, exposed to lose it almost as easily as these Protestants are to acquire it.

"The day after we reached Logansport, a rapidly improving town on the Canal that is nearly completed, and will unite the Wabash with the Maumee at Fort Wayne, and thus Lake Erie with the Ohio, and the Mississippi through the States of Indiana and Illinois. I found there a good number of Catholics, and promised to send them one of the first Priests I could obtain. I said Mass the next morning, and then left for home, yet some days' journey, passing through Fayetteville, Attica, Covington, Terre Haute, &c. Few Catholics are as yet collected in these growing towns, but soon there will be more. Had I said Mass at Terre Haute about 20 Catholics might have been present, and many Protestants joining them, and in our new country that is a sufficient indication to send a missionary. By this very visit to Europe I trust to obtain some, whom I will be able to support with the generous gift of the Association, and thus place Terre Haute and many other such towns on the line of missionary round. I have myself heard in the city of Baltimore the interesting account of those who remembered to have Mass said in their room by a Missionary, there being no resident Pastor; Baltimore, where now five parish Churches, one splendid Cathedral, one Seminary, and five private Chapels in the different Communities and Hospitals, make twelve sanctuaries in which the 21 priests, living with their Archbishop in that metropolis, officiate. Poor Diocese of Vincennes! Let us, however, put trust in God, and what a change can a few years, through His Blessing and the perseverance of zealous souls, effect.

"Shortly after my return, Mr. Lalumière came home, and the account of his journey was very consoling. He had found more Catholics than I had, and many places ready to receive a priest. In three places they had begun to build Churches. At Fort Wayne they were finishing one, 60 feet by 30, and the Congregation numbers 150 Catholic families. I was happy to send them the Rev. M. Ruff, from Metz in France, recently ordained, and speaking the three languages used there, French, English, and German. Of the latter there are a good many living there and in the environs. I had ordained Mr. Ruff Subdeacon and Deacon before my journey to Chicago, and had sent him to the Seminary of St. Louis (St. Mary of the Barrens) to make his retreat, and there he was ordained priest by that excellent prelate, Dr. Rosati.

"We have as yet no Seminary, no College, no religious establishment in any part of the Diocese, except an academy and school kept in Vincennes by four Sisters of Charity from the House of Nazareth in Kentucky. They had been recalled to Nazareth some months before I came. My first care was to secure their return, and they resumed their school the end of last April. When I left they had four boarders and about fifty day scholars."

As soon as he arrived at his Diocese, he perceived immediately that, in order to provide for its urgent wants, it would be necessary to obtain Priests from Europe—the harvest was already ripe, or rather was perishing for want of some one to gather it in, and it would not do to wait until they had found or raised up labourers from among themselves. He determined, however, to make the above described visitation in order to understand the extent and exact nature of its necessities from personal observation. In his Letters to his friends, describing his journey, he enters into many details, which are omitted in his communication to the Leopoldine Association, as not becoming the gravity of what may be regarded as an official document.[55]

[55] In one Letter he speaks of having travelled 550 miles on horseback during the last six weeks. He describes very graphically the little groups of emigrants whom he fell in with, exploring the country and seeking for new homes—his conversation with them and the scattered residents, taking advantage of every opportunity, in a quiet, unobtrusive manner, to do away with their prejudices in regard to the Catholic Church, and to instruct them in its real doctrines and principles. Wherever he heard of a Catholic family, he spared evidently no labour or fatigue to find them out and

But in all of them there is not a word of murmuring or an expression of discouragement. His whole life had been an act of conscientious and ever-increasing self-devotion, and the difficulties which now stood in his way only served to increase his zeal and activity. As soon as he had made himself acquainted with the condition of his Diocese, he immediately took the necessary steps to provide for its wants so far as was in his power. His heart instinctively turned to his own country in the hour of need, and he again crossed the ocean to seek for missionaries and for such pecuniary help as would enable him to finish his Cathedral and provide schools for the education of the young. His notes and memoranda indicate that he found himself very much out of place in the courts and among the grand personages with whom his office and the object of his journey brought him in contact. He was received, however, everywhere with the greatest kindness.[56] He took advantage of the opportunity

visit them, and his descriptions of their lonely situation in the then wilderness are very touching. Sometimes it is a poor negro, with his family, emigrants from Maryland or Kentucky, living in the woods, all crowding to the door to welcome the Bishop and get his blessing. Sometimes a respectable white family, brought up amid Catholic privileges, now without Priest, or Mass, or Catholic neighbors, and often exhibiting the sad effects of such privations. No wonder that the poor Bishop's heart sometimes almost sank within him, and that he often exclaimed, as in a Letter to Bishop David, in mingled Latin and French, "Ostium magnum apertum —moyens nul à present."

[56] The late Empress of Austria, and Prince Metternich in particular, took the liveliest interest in providing for the wants of the new Diocese of Vincennes, and loaded the good Bishop with kindnesses of every sort.

to visit the 'Limina Apostolorum' and to receive for himself and his Diocese the benediction of the common Father of the Faithful, and then hastened back to his home in the wilderness.

A warm welcome awaited him on his return to his Episcopal City, for all alike, Protestants as well as Catholics, had become very much attached to their good Bishop. And now commenced a new series of labours which were to end only with his life, which was drawing to its close. With the resources which had been placed at his disposal in Europe, he established a Diocesan College Seminary in his Episcopal City, an Orphan Asylum and a Free School. The surplus was spent in finishing his Cathedral[57] and in helping to erect small Churches at certain points where they were most needed.

He brought twenty Priests and Seminarians with him from France,[58] but though his health had already

[57] " Besides, we are completely upside down with our Church repairs. The Sanctuary unroofed, the nave and aisles a forest of scaffolding for the plastering, then the steeple is to be got up—the wood already cut at St. Francisville, and soon to sail up our proud Wabash, and go and tell the skies, not a lie, as the tall column in London, but the true love of Vincennes for the honour of God."—*Letter to Rev. Mr. Shaw, Aug.*, 1838.

[58] As we have seen, when he arrived in his Diocese there were but three Priests in the whole of it, and one of these merely lent to him. In 1839, the year of his death, the Catholic Almanac makes the following recapitulation of the State of the Diocese :

Churches, - - - - -	23	Religious Communities, - -	2
Church Buildings, - - -	6	Theological Seminary, - -	1
Stations occasionally visited, -	28	College for young men, - -	1
Clergymen on the Mission, -	22	Female Academy, - - -	1
Clergymen otherwise employed,	2	Free Schools, - - - -	2

begun to fail,[69] he still performed the work of one in the vigour and freshness of early manhood. At home, he was at once the Bishop, the Pastor of the Congregation, the Professor of Theology for his Seminary, and a Teacher for one of his Academies. He wrote twice a month to every Priest in his Diocese, and thus communicated to them a portion of that zeal for the glory of God and the salvation of souls which formed the constant object of his every thought and action. He visited every portion of his Diocese repeatedly, and wherever he went he engaged in all the duties of an ordinary Pastor. Indiana and Illinois had at this time, as is well known, embarked largely in that immense system of internal improvements which, for the time being, ended so disastrously. The labourers upon them, mostly Irish Emigrants, suffered greatly from the cholera and malignant fevers. One of the great af-

[69] He caught a severe cold while riding on the outside of a stage coach in Ohio, on his way to the Council at Baltimore in 1837, which ended in a confirmed consumption. Bishop Bruté was tall in stature and thin, but naturally very strong and vigorous. Recreation in the ordinary sense of the word he never took, but on holydays and during the hours of recreation at the College, he would often spend a portion of the time in making paths among the woods, and in erecting a sort of Chapel on the mountain side, which was known as the Grotto. His features were plain, but his face was full of intelligence, and marked by that peculiar sweetness of expression which has been often noticed in the countenances of very holy persons—a sort of celestial radiance which came from the pure and holy soul within, and which often made a vivid impression upon those who approached him. He would never permit his likeness to be taken, and the only portrait of him which exists was from a cast taken after his death. It gives a very good representation of his features.

flictions which Bishop Bruté had to suffer was being unable to provide for the spiritual wants of these poor people, whose lively faith and generous, impulsive nature had attached him very warmly to them. He often went among them himself—heard their Confessions—celebrated Mass for them in their miserable cabins, and prepared the sick and dying for the awful passage to eternity. In the words of Dr. McCaffrey, "Difficulties that would have disheartened almost any one else, only served to increase his zeal and charity. Having commenced a journey of four hundred miles in such a state of bodily suffering that he could not sit upright on his horse, he nevertheless completed it without the intermission of a single day. Shortly before his death, he left Vincennes to visit a distant mission, which he had already visited thrice within the year, and though so weak and attenuated that he could scarcely support his tottering frame, in the absence of the Pastor he attended to three distant sick-calls on the same day, and, almost dying, administered the consolations of religion to those who appeared no nearer mortal dissolution than himself." It was the same with him until the last moment.[60] His resolute will and fervent zeal seemed

[60] To judge from his Letters, the thought of rest or retirement never seems to have entered into his mind, or, if it did, he put it away from him —thus writing to Mr. Shaw in 1838, when, broken down by sickness, the vision of a quiet upper room in a friend's (Mr. Blenkinsop's) house passes across his mind, and for a moment he indulges the wish that he might be

to triumph over painful and debilitating disease, which was destroying his body; and when no longer able to work himself, he cheered on those who were engaged in the task with words full of courage and enthusiasm. His Letters at this period also bring still more strongly in relief, on account of his inability to labour himself, a point in his character for which he had always been remarkable—his kind consideration for others. It seemed to grieve him to give orders without being able to take his share of the labor necessary to carry them into execution.[61] Among the Priests of his Diocese at this time was the Rev. Michael Shaw,[62] a convert to the Catholic Church, who had formerly, I

permitted to rest there until death; but he immediately checks himself, and adds: "But shame! non recuso laborem."

[61] This activity was not merely the effect of temperament, but rather the result of his zeal and dislike of slothfulness. Naturally, he was fond of retirement and study. He invariably rose after his first sleep. If he felt drowsy afterwards, he would say, as if addressing his body, "If you want more sleep, you must take it the next time you get a chance."—*Rev. Mr. Hickey.*

[62] The Rev. Mr. Shaw erected the first Church at Madison, Ind. The difficulties he had to encounter, judging from the Bishop's answers to his Letters, must have been very great. The Bishop was evidently much attached to this good Priest, and did all he could to aid and encourage him. The following little note, written on a scrap of paper and addressed to Mr. Shaw, is characteristic of Bp. Bruté—of his lively faith and sympathy with the feelings of others: "St. George's Day, 1838. How many associations! from the days of St. Paul and Lucius—of St. George and Saint Alban—St. Austin—the Venerable Bede—St. Edward—and the innumerable Saints of fifteen ages, to the days of Fisher and More and Mary, and the glorious victims of our divine Faith—to those of our Milner and Lingard, and the host of able and fervent restorers of its glories for England.

"The mind and heart dwell to-day, in this land of hope and promise—and mine earnestly so, my dear Sir, in union with yours. The days of

believe, been an officer in the British army. I have in my possession a large number of Notes and Letters which the good Bishop wrote to him during the last years of his life. They are entirely unstudied —written upon the spur of the moment, but are full of interest, not only as exhibiting all the beautiful traits of his character—his lively faith, his active usefulness, and his ardent zeal—but also as giving an insight into the nature of his administration. It was characterized, as I have remarked, by the most untiring energy and perseverance. No good work once undertaken was ever allowed to stand still; and it is impossible to understand how so much was done in so short a time, especially as most of it was accomplished while the States of Illinois and Indiana were labouring under the most severe financial embarrassments.[63]

such praise to God in Bangor and Croyland and Winchester, &c. &c.—the holy Victim offered everywhere is present to both of us. Accept, dear friend, these remembrances of the day . . . . of the Faith—Memoriam fecit miribilium suorum."

With all his tender affection, however, for Mr. Shaw, he was very careful not to allow any fault to go unreproved; thus in another Letter he writes to him: "I cannot forbear, my beloved brother and son in Christ, chiding you for one sentence you have allowed to escape you, and which is not according to order. 'I am *willing*,' you say, 'to serve Madison as long as Mr. ——— is legitimately occupied in making collections under your authority, but I am not willing to stay here, merely to enable him to run about the country at his own pleasure, and neglect every duty connected with his charge.' Alas! my dear friend, we are all obliged in this world to fulfil the duties of our charge, with all care and affection for it, for God's sake, even in sight of others not so faithful as they ought to be."

[63] What makes it the more wonderful is, that the Bishop seems to have

But at length the poor body, to which he had given little rest for so many years, refused to do its work any longer. I cannot better describe the closing scenes of his eventful and well-spent life than in the words of the beautiful discourse from which I have so often quoted. Its author received the details from the mouths of those who had witnessed them. "Death," he says, "which could be no unwelcome visitor to one whose thoughts, hopes, and affections all centred in a better world, found him full-handed of good works, and longing only to be dissolved and to be with Christ. Invincibly patient and resigned under the severest suffering, full of tender piety, calm, collected, and brightly exhibiting his characteristic virtues to the last, he set a beautiful example of the manner in which a Christian should prepare himself to run his final race and to win the Crown of a glorious immortality. As his strength diminished, his devotion increased. He sought no alleviation for his sufferings: on the con-

had a great horror of running into debt, and would sign no mortgage upon Church Property. The assistance he received from Europe enabled him to carry out for a while these good resolutions; but if he had lived a few years longer, he would probably have found himself obliged to modify them somewhat. Personally, he cared nothing about money. As Father Hickey said to Mr. Miles, "If he had five dollars in his pocket, it went to the first person who asked for it." His clothes were always very plain, and he often gave away everything except what he had upon his back; and even these were not safe, for he has been known repeatedly to take off his linen and underclothes and give them to the poor negroes whom he was accustomed to visit.

trary, he was eager still to labour and endure, in the twofold view of doing good to others and resembling more his crucified Saviour. When unable to walk or stand, he would at least sit up, and write to any whom he could hope to benefit by his correspondence; and to those around him he would speak on pious subjects, such as the love of God, conformity to His Holy Will, or devotion to the Blessed Virgin, with the unction of a Saint and the ardour of a Seraph. But six hours before his death, he wrote with his own hand, and not without much difficulty and pain, several moving letters to persons who had unfortunately abandoned the practice of their faith, and to whom he wished to make this dying appeal in behalf of their souls, while the portals of eternity were closing upon him.[64] These last precious days of his life were thus entirely taken up in works of Charity, in instructing, edifying, and consoling those who were with him, and in intimate and affectionate Communion with his God, whom he hoped soon to see face to face, and to love and enjoy forever. He preferred often to be left alone, that he might the more freely indulge his pious feelings, and for this end he would allow no one to watch by him at

[64] I have in my possession a Letter to Bp. Flaget, and another to the late B. U. Campbell, Esq., to whom he was always very much attached, dictated after he had received the last Sacraments and signed by himself with the trembling hand of death.

night, until his mortal agony had begun. When his friends affectionately sought to know what they could do to relieve his sufferings, he would answer them by pointing out some passage of Sacred Scripture, or Chapter of the Following of Christ, which he desired them to read to him, or by asking them to say some prayers for his happy death. No agonies of pain could extort from him a single expression of distress. 'The will of God be done,' was the constant language of his lips, as it was the abiding sentiment of his heart. When preparing to receive the holy Viaticum, he wrote to us in the true spirit of saintly humility, requesting the prayers of our Seminary and of the Sisterhood, and begging pardon for whatever offences or bad example he had ever given to any one at either institution. A few days before his dissolution the strength of his naturally vigorous constitution rallied for a time, and his physician promised him at least a temporary recovery: he told the physician he was mistaken, and, whether he knew it supernaturally or otherwise, named the exact time of his approaching departure. He gave himself the orders for preparing his grave, and as calmly directed the modes of sepulture, and proper rites to be observed, as if he was discharging an ordinary duty. On the morning of the day before his death he remarked to the clergyman, who attended him with unwearied solicitude and affection: 'My dear child, I have the whole day yet to stay with you; to-morrow with God!' To another pious friend he used these simple but expressive words: 'I am going home.' Heaven was indeed his home; he had always so regarded it; there was his treasure; his heart was there; he had ever longed to be with God, and 'see Him as He is'; and now the door of the Father's House was opening to him, and Angels were on the wing to meet his departing spirit and conduct it to its place of rest. He was happy, therefore, amid the pangs and terrors of death; for he trusted that he was but going home. After having received the last Sacrament, he directed the departing prayers to be recited, which he answered devoutly and fervently until the last, and then on the morning of the 26th of June, at half-past one o'clock, he calmly and sweetly surrendered his soul into the hands of his Creator.

. . . .

"His death was deplored as a general calamity. He was especially lamented by the poor, the widow and orphan. The people of Vincennes felt that they had lost a public benefactor, and his own flock, both clergy and laity, bewailed, as well they might, the death of such a Pastor. All, with one accord, mourned for the scholar, the philanthropist, and the saint. Crowds of persons of every rank, and of all denominations, visited his corpse and assisted at the ceremonies of his burial. The Mayor and civic authorities, and learned Societies of Vincennes passed resolutions to attend his funeral. The whole population poured forth to accompany, in solemn silence, his honoured remains to their last resting-place on earth." [65]

According to custom, his body was buried under the Sanctuary of his Cathedral.[66] The memory of

[65] Discourse by Revd. Dr. McCaffrey, *ut supra.*

[66] I cannot refrain from inserting here, though without his permission, a portion of a Letter which I lately received from the Revd. E. Audran, Pastor of the Cathedral of Vincennes, in answer to my request for a copy of the inscription on the Bishop's tomb:

VINCENNES, July 31st, 1860.

Right Rev. Sir:

. . . .

"Bishop Bruté was first buried under the Sanctuary of the present Cathedral. In the month of November, 1840, the floor of the Sanctuary having been raised and the whole ground under it dug out to make room for a subterranean chapel, the body was removed and placed immediately behind the Altar of this chapel. It has remained there ever since.

"The following is the inscription on the wall above his tomb. Bishop Rosati wrote it:

"Hic jacet Simon Gabriel Bruté, Episcopus Vincennensis. Primitus Rhedonis in Galliis XII kal. Ap. MDCCLXXIX. Humanioribus litteris in patria, Severioribus in Parisiensi Academia, et tandem Divinis in Celeberrimo S. Sulpitii Seminario operam felicissimam dedit.

"Inter Olerii discipulos annumeratus religionis propagandæ desiderio flagrans ex Galliis Americam navigavit Anno MDCCCX. Hic Juventutis institutioni addictus Baltimorensi S. Mariæ Collegio primum prœfuit. Tum in monte S. Mariæ ad Emmittsburgum adolescentibus iis præsertim qui in Sorte Dñi vocantur humanis et Ecclesiasticis disciplinis verbo et exemplo excolendis indefessus incubuit.

"A Gregorio XVI Pontifice Maximo ad Vincennopolitanam Sedem nuper erectam omnibus acclamantibus appellatus, humilis Christi discipulus solis suis oculis vilis ut pastorale munus susciperet adduci vix potuit. In Ecclesia Cathedrali S. Ludovici Episcopus inunctus et consecratus V kal. Nov. MDCCCXXXIV novam Diocesim solus perlustravit. Operarios evangelicos ad illam excolendam adsciscendi gratia in Europam profectus illinc lectissima sacerdotum caterva stipatus reversus, vineam sibi concreditam,

"good Bishop Bruté," as he is always called, had not been dimmed by time. Those who knew him, and who were trained to virtue by his precepts and example, love to speak of him, to repeat his words, and to tell the incidents of his saintly life. Of all the holy missionaries whom God has from time to time sent to plant the seeds of Faith in this new country no name is more often repeated, no labours are more often dwelt upon, than his, and thus the undying influence of his beautiful example still helps on the good cause to which his life was devoted—the salvation of souls and the greater glory of God.

plantare, colere, irrigare, ampliare, defendere modis omnibus, verbo, opere, scriptis, laboribus, sudoribus, ad extremum usque vitæ, quam pro ovibus suis bonus pastor impendit non cessavit.

"Supremum diem obiit VI kal. Junii MDCCCXXXIX.

"The removal of the body took place privately at six o'clock in the morning—none being present but his successor the Rt. Rev. Bishop De la Hailandiere, who performed the office laid down in the ritual for the occasion, and a few ecclesiastics and religious. I was present. A feeling of pious veneration and a desire to know what had become of the mortal remains of the saintly man whose angelical virtues were still perfuming all round us, impelled us to open the simple wooden coffin. But the decay was complete; and although but little more than a year had elapsed since his death, the vestments which adhered yet to a skeleton could alone recall to the mind something of his outward form. We closed the coffin in silence, and remembered that it was humility he loved above all.

"Lying by his side, on the right hand of the Altar, is the body of the Right Rev. Stephen Bazin, third Bishop of Vincennes.

"Respectfully yours,

"in our Lord J. C.

"E. AUDRAN, pt."

Aeternitas.

SKETCHES

OF THE

FRENCH REVOLUTION.

"*Nos insensati vitam illorum æstimabamus insaniam, et finem illorum sine honore: ecce, quomodo computati sunt inter filios Dei, et inter sanctos sors illorum est.*"—LIB. SAP., *Cap.* V. 4, 5.

SOME BRIEF NOTES

Of my Recollections connected with the Persecution in France in 1793, *and the following Years.*

BEING a boy of fourteen years of age in 1793, I was often sent by my family to attend the tribunals which were sitting in our City of Rennes, to witness and bring back information in regard to the trials of our priests. On account of the excessive terror which prevailed, and the fear of betraying themselves to danger, by manifesting their feelings amid the savage mob which generally attended them, grown-up people dared not go. I myself never had the courage to follow the victims to the scaffold, but I went to the tribunals. There were at this time three tribunals sitting, sometimes the same day, and sending their victims to the Guillotine, or the Fusillade, viz.: the regular Criminal Court, to which generally the priests were sent; the Revolutionary Tribunal, which took cognizance chiefly of the so-called political conspirators, and before which few Ecclesiastics were brought—I do not remember to have attended any there—and the Military Commission, where those taken in arms or about the place of some encounter were judged. Once I witnessed there the trial of a Brother of the Christian Schools. The three tribunals did not, however, observe any very strict limits of jurisdiction; but I seldom attended others than the Criminal Court. When I assisted at the trial of these holy victims, I could repeat almost word for word the various questions and answers; and I have often regretted that I did not write them down at the time—but, in truth, I dared not do it—for so oppressive was the fear of keeping any memoranda, which in the frequent and sudden domiciliary visits might have been found, that the most valuable and interesting papers, and even printed documents, were destroyed—especially in families exposed to suspicion and danger, as on many accounts ours was. I remember that, wishing to preserve a copy of the Testament of Louis XVI., I put it into a bottle well corked and sealed, and buried it in the ground; but when a long time after I dug it up, the wet had found its way into the bottle and nearly destroyed the paper. Afterwards when, in better times, I ought to have written my recollections, I trusted to my memory, and deferred doing so. And now (1818) that at last I have made the attempt, in these notes, to record and fix my remembrances, I find that a great deal has passed away from my mind, or become to a certain degree confused and uncertain. I have written, however, the following pages, as correctly as was in my power, and have recorded the circumstances exactly as they occurred, and were witnessed either by myself, or told to me at the time by those who had every opportunity of being well informed. It would be very difficult for me to convey to others anything but a general idea of our situation and the impressions we were under at that time. As I gather up my scattered remembrances, the whole comes back to me very vividly, and I may be said to *feel* as I did then; but it would be impossible for others to put themselves mind and heart into our place, and realize what was the habitual condition of Catholics at that time. During the progress of the persecution, the greater number of the Priests of the Diocese had been either guillotined or shot, or transported to the penal colonies. The more aged and infirm were imprisoned in the Castle of Mount Saint Michael (about 50 miles from Rennes). Of the few left, in deep concealment, some were almost daily discovered, and, according to the *Law*, led, with those who had harboured them, to the guillotine within twenty-four hours. All the Churches of the Diocese had been seized upon and converted to profane uses.[1] Some were used as storehouses for forage, hay, etc.; some were converted into *casernes* and stables; some into

[1] I find the following memorandum on a loose sheet of paper among Bishop Bruté's manuscripts:

Churches of Rennes before and after the Revolution.

1. The Cathedral St. Melanie,* first Bishop of Rennes, an old, vast, high-towering building—an abbey founded on this spot in the 6th century—during the Revolution turned into a stable for the cavalry, the steps leading to the grand entrance having been removed, and a sloping way made for the horses, immense heaps of manure, &c., piled up on both sides of the public square; the soldiers in their shirt-sleeves going out and coming in, and at work about the horses, with continued oaths and vile songs, some of them in mockery of the offices of the Church—manifesting their coarse impiety in every possible way.

2. Toussaint, All-Saints'—the largest and most beautiful church in the city, turned into a stable—was burnt one day, with forty horses and some of the men; the ruins cleared away, a public square now where it stood.

3. St. Martin—pulled down; a garden occupies the spot, and a house in the corner of the church-yard.

4. St. Hélier's.—This church, standing by itself, was turned into a powder-magazine, the windows being closed up with mason-work; since repaired and restored to the use of the parishioners.

5. St. Stephen's—made a depot for the wagons of the army, and a shop for repairing them; still standing, but utterly desolate.

6. St. John's—also turned into a shop for the workmen of the army. The whole interior was so completely destroyed that it has never been restored to the use of Religion. It is at present occupied by the public stages (messageries) of the city.

7. St. George's.—Used as a stable for cavalry; since, part has been demolished, and part left standing in a ruinous condition.

* It appears from the History of Rennes that St. Peter's was the ancient Cathedral of Rennes. In the Plan of the City, as given in D'Argentré's History of Brittany, 1616, it is thus stated:—St. Melanie's Church and Abbey was at that time outside of the walls. St. Melanie was not the first Bishop of Rennes. The first whose existence is well ascertained was named Febedíolus, an. 459; the second, Anthemius; the third, St. Amand; St. Melanie was the fourth. He died in 530. The Church, or rather Cathedral, of St. Peter's, afterwards became dilapidated, and was taken down, and the Abbey church of St. Melanie was made the Cathedral.

manufactories, and some altered into dwelling-houses by those who bought them; some were levelled with the ground in order that the materials

8 St. Germain—was turned into a *caserne*, and then into a depot of artillery; it was filled for many years with cannons, cannon carriages, &c.; now repaired and restored to the use of the parishioners.

9. St. Sauveur's.—Made the Temple of Reason, and resounded with all the vile and blasphemous speeches of the times; afterwards restored to religious uses.

10. St. Laurent's.—Long neglected and almost in ruins; at length repaired and restored. It was in this church I married my brother to his good wife.

So much for the parish churches. As regards the convents and religious houses:

11. The Convent of the Cordeliers was turned into a stable for the cavalry, then into a depot of wagons; finally part of it was restored and given to the Seminary.

12. The Convent of the Carmelites.—Levelled to the ground; a street.

13. The Convent of the Minims.—Bought by an architect, who turned it into an elegant house.

14. The Convent of the Augustins.—The general blacksmith's shop of the army; since restored, and serves for the parish of St. Stephen.

15. The Jacobins.—The bake-house for the army; still abandoned and half in ruins.

16. The Capuchins—became a private dwelling with its fine walks and shades.

17. The discalced Carmelites.—A private store-house.

18. St. Aubin (a parish church)—turned into a stable, then into a store; half ruined, afterwards restored.

19. The Visitation—turned into a store and private dwelling-house.

20. The Second Visitation—into the Grand Masonic Hall.

21. The Ursulines—A barrack; half destroyed.

22. The Second Ursulines—the house of a notorious Atheist.

23. The Trinity—Convent of Refuge, into a prison.

24. The Good Shepherd—another house of refuge; also into a prison.

25. The House of Retreat—a barrack for soldiers.

26. The Diocesan Seminary—into a hospital for the soldiers.

27. The Preparatory Seminary—a barrack.

28. St. Cyr—into a hospital for foul diseases of the wicked.

29. The Grand Hospital—turned into a school and depot of artillery.

30. The Mother House of the Sisters of Charity—sold.

might be sold, or to make room for new streets: some, in short, were turned to the worst of purposes (yet under Providence, by this means, preserved); changed into temples for the *decadi*, the festivals of the national calendar, so curious a thing by itself, or for the clubs and political assemblies of the time. All the old and best families, the most zealous for Religion, were not only deprived of all public exercise of it, but were scarcely able to practise their private and secret devotions in the interior of their houses. It was forbidden by law, and under penalties of fine and imprisonment, to observe Sunday or to distinguish it in any way from common days, whilst the *decadi*, or every tenth day, which had been substituted for the Sunday and made the *legal* day of rest, was under the same penalties enforced, by ceasing from labor, keeping the shops closed, &c. Such a state of things, which was the habitual condition of the whole population from the end of 1792 until 1795, had brought the minds of those

31. The House of the Daughters of Wisdom—sold.

32, 33. The two Houses of the Brothers of the Poor Schools—sold.

34. The House of the Confraternity of Notre Dame—turned into a store-house, afterwards into a stable.

35. The Chapel of St. James—into a store for toys, then into a dwelling-house.

36. St. Ives, Hospital—preserved but long shut up.

37. St. Yves, where the Canons officiated—into a store.

38. The Hospital of the Incurables—preserved, but no chapel permitted.

39. The Calvary—into a place of meeting for the Revolutionary Club, a store, and then a theatre.

who still remained attached to their Faith into a most desponding state in regard to the future prospects of religion in France. This was peculiarly the case at certain periods of increasing darkness, when those who exercised authority in our unhappy country manifested their intention of rooting out every vestige of the ancient Faith. It would be impossible now to recall fully the painful impressions of those times, or to make them sensible to those who did not pass through that strange ordeal. I have endeavored to give a sketch of our Sundays, as I remember them, at my dear mother's, who so resolutely did all that was in her power to preserve us to Religion for those *better days* which she never ceased confidently to anticipate. I could relate many curious things in regard to the profane celebration of the Festivals of *Reason*, as they were called. The *Age of Reason*, as Paine calls it, was, as they hoped, fully established in our France, and every *decadi* was *sanctified* by some new invention. I can still see with my mind's eye the curious processions which they made through the streets of the city on those days, going to the Temple of Reason. They were composed of youths on the Festival of *Youth*—of hoary men, picked up for the purpose, on the Festival of *Old Age*—of husbandmen, carrying with them the implements of agriculture, on the Festival of *Agriculture*—of mechanics with their tools, on the days of the *Arts*. In the month of "Fructidor" they had exhibitions of Fruits and of the various returns of the harvest, in their special times, &c., &c. Now it all seems like a dream, and these exhibitions and processions have a ridiculous effect, as seen through the faint memory of them. Those who had established them supposed that they would accustom the multitude to do without Religion, except the religion of nature, as they called it. As each Decadi came around, they endeavoured to make it more attractive by new inventions of pompous shows, or philosophical and sentimental exhibitions, mixing up with them special ovations and songs, civic banquets and public games, copied from the old Greek and Roman Republics. The first year, and first round of these profane and systematic attempts to root out the Christian Religion from the hearts of the people and make them Infidels, went on with such a continual supply of novelty and interest, for the multitude, that it made an impression which now it would be difficult to estimate correctly. Even then, however, the effect was often very ridiculous, and as the repetition of each Decadi proved more forced and tiresome, it became dark and hopeless, as the times were the best mark by which we could measure the slow but certain return of the old and true Religion, and the failure of this impious scheme —self-defeated—as it proved. The thought, the very memory of those miserable exhibitions, has vanished away. For instance, the Festival of Divorce! Who now can form an idea of the manner in which it was celebrated? It was on one of the Decadi, at the Temple of Reason—a Player from the Theatre, the Orator of the day. I have in my possession his discourse in print—all furious nonsense against Religion, and its oppression of our *liberty*, in making marriage indissoluble, &c. These things are gone and forgotten, but the admirable virtues then displayed by those holy Confessors who remained faithful to their religion will live through eternity, in the heavenly records.

It was my object in the following pages to record some of those scenes of fidelity and Christian heroism, as memory brought them back to me. After I had written them out (in 1818) I found that several of them had also been recorded by the Abbé Carron.[2] But how many cases are not recorded in his precious Memoirs! The first one, for instance, which I have sketched, that of M. Raoul, and of which I was a witness. The drawing which accompanies it presents an exact picture of the scene at the Tribunal, or very nearly so; although at this moment it is nearly 27 years ago, yet it is as vivid in my mind as if I was still there,

[2] The work of the Abbé Carron here alluded to is, "Les Confesseurs de la Foi dans l'Eglise Gallicane, a la fin du dix huitième Siècle," 4 vols. 12mo, Paris, 1820. I have gathered from it some additional particulars in regard to confessors mentioned in the following pages, and placed them in the notes.

boy as I then was, standing behind and leaning upon the seat of the holy Confessor, with nothing but the railing of the Tribunal between us—my poor heart beating so violently all the time.

Trial of the Priest and the three Sisters of La Chapelle St. Aubert, Diocese of Rennes.

"Mr. Raoul, and the three good Sisters of La Chapelle St. Aubert, have been seized and brought to the city yesterday; to-day they are to be tried." Such was the sad news of the morning, and about 8 or 9 o'c. I saw them passing under our windows on their way to the Tribunal, followed by the mob, who accompanied them with the usual cry, "à la Guillotine." I immediately went after them, and, young as I was, crept along from place to place until I got so near that I stood immediately behind M. Raoul seated upon the bench, with my arms folded upon the railing, almost touching his back. The Sisters were seated upon a bench across the other side of the floor. The Judges elevated with their seats upon a higher floor, about upon a level with the heads of the Prisoners, and the Gendarmes. The President of the Court was Bouassier, who had been a reputable attorney of Rennes, esteemed before the Revolution as a good, moral man, but a philosopher, as our French Deists were called; naturally kind-hearted, but gradually drawn on, or rather pushed on from one excess to another, and then fixed in his dreadful position by personal fear. "Thy name and age," said the President. "Raoul-Bodin" (not certain of the second name),[3] answered the Priest, aged 70 years, or perhaps more, I do not exactly remember, but I still see the worthy man, as he sat there, tall, very thin, with a bald forehead, hair quite gray, a placid, noble, and truly religious countenance. "Thy profession?" "A Priest—Curé of La Chapelle St. Aubert." "Didst thou take the civic oath?"[4] "No, citizen." "Why not?" was then asked; and he answered "because he could not, according to his conscientious views of the subject." Two or three short questions and answers may then have taken place which I do not call to mind, but I remember distinctly that the good old man began

[3] "I cannot recall the name—it was Raoul, or Craoul-mell; but it has faded from my memory."—*Note by Bp. Bruté.* It appears from Tresvaux, "Histoire," &c. vol. ii. p. 114, that his name was Raoul-Bodin, as Bp. Bruté first wrote it. The name of the noble and charitable ladies who perished with him was La Gracière. There were two other Priests concealed in their house, who escaped. They were denounced to the authorities by a Tiler from Fougéres, who saw the Priests when mending the roof. The inhabitants of Chapelle St. Aubert would have rescued Mr. Raoul from the Gendarmes when they arrested him, but he dissuaded them. M. Tresvaux says that his memory is still venerated in that place. They were put to death on the 8th of October, 1794.

[4] The oath to the civil Constitution of the Clergy, as mentioned at p. 27.

to entreat in favour of the three Sisters in whose house he had been arrested—speaking in a very calm but very affecting and impressive manner, to the President and the court, for two or three minutes, until he was repeatedly silenced. The tones of his voice are still sounding in my ears; his words were to this effect: "Citizens, judges! will you put to death these poor ladies, for an act of hospitality so inoffensive to the public—so natural, so worthy of their kind hearts, when I had been for twenty years (or more) their Pastor? Do spare them, citizens; it becomes so much better the Republic to show clemency," &c. "Silence! They must speak for themselves. Silence! It is none of thy office to address the Tribunal in their favour. Silence! citizen." He was compelled to stop, and sat down (he had stood up whilst speaking) and looked towards the poor Sisters, who were then, successively, called upon to give their names and age, and acknowledge that they knew the Priest and gave him asylum in contravention to the national decrees. They were three elderly Sisters, between 45 and 50 years of age, or more, of a most respectable and gentle appearance and dress—a calm, simple deportment before the Tribunal. They lived on their estate at Chapelle St. Aubert. One of them had been a Religious, expelled by the decrees of the Convention from her Convent, and obliged to return and live with her Sisters. She was now

LIBERTE
EGALITE
ET
FRATERNI
OU
LA MOR
REPUBLIQUE
UNE
ET INDIVISIBLE
OU
LA MORT.
LE PEUPLE FRANCAIS
RECONNOIT L'EXISTENCE
DE
L'ETRE SUPREME ET
L'IMMORTALITE
DE L'AME.

f 120

dressed like them, and seated the last in order upon the bench, and was the last called upon to answer. In addition to the replies made by her Sisters to the interrogatories of the Judges, she added, "That she had no home after her expulsion from her Convent, and was compelled to return to her Sisters and live upon their bounty, and that consequently she did not come under the severe terms of the law against those who gave protection to Priests." The plea seemed fair enough, but it gave occasion to no particular consultation amongst the Judges, but was immediately overruled, in a very harsh and abusive manner, as a preposterous and useless attempt to have her cause separated from that of the others.

She then, if I am not mistaken, or one of the Sisters, began to entreat in favour of the good old man, as he had done for them, but in a more earnest and severe manner. "How cruel it would be to put to death so holy and innocent a man, who had committed no crime, but whose whole life had been spent in doing good to all, and especially to those who were then called the 'Sans-culottes,' so particularly dear to the Republic, to the poor, to the aged, to the little ones," &c. She was repeatedly ordered to be silent, but became only the more animated, until compelled to hold her peace, and let the matter take its course.

The examination of all four of them had occupied but a short time—being, in fact, a mere formality, since the Letter of the Law was most express, "the Priest and those who harbour him to be put to death within twenty-four hours after being seized."

The President then proceeded, after scarcely a moment's conference with the other Judges, to apply this cruel enactment, and to pass sentence of death, in the name of the Republic, upon the Priest Raoul and the three Sisters who had given him asylum—adding the usual order, that all the religious objects found in the house, and which in the language of the sentence were styled "les hochets[5] du fanatisme," should be previously burned at the side of the scaffold.

When the sentence had been pronounced the Nun could not restrain her feelings of indignation. She rose from her seat, snatched from her cap the national cockade, which even the women were obliged to wear during these days of delusion, and, trampling it under her feet, she addressed alternately the Judges and the people with two or three sentences of vehement reproach: "Barbarous people!" she exclaimed, "amongst what savage nations has hospitality ever been made a crime, punishable with death?" I cannot now call to mind her other expressions, except that she appealed to the higher tribunal of God, and denounced his judgment against them.

[5] Hochets—Children's playthings.

Her Sisters tried in the meanwhile to check her, and recall her to silence. The one who sat next to her pulled gently at her dress (I can see her now), as if urging her to stop.

All was soon hushed to silence, and the Judge addressed, as usual, an emphatic and opprobrious charge to the victims, and particularly the Priest, with bitter reproaches for their fanaticism, as he called it—addressing himself also to the spectators with energetic declarations of their determined resolution to free the Republic from all dangers, and have the Priests and their accomplices and dupes brought to the same punishment; the whole a most shocking piece of outrage, and raving enthusiasm still more shocking, as coming from one who, like the unfortunate Bouassier, had enjoyed a character little fitted for such a horrid profanation of every best principle.

During the whole time M. Raoul was engaged in prayer. Methinks I can still hear the sounds, and low, little swellings of his prayer—some of the Psalms, it seemed from the Latin final or syllable, rising from time to time in a half-suppressed murmur—whilst the Jailer or Executioner (for he was always present) was putting on the handcuffs, and securing them so tight that I remember the Priest gave signs of uneasiness, and looked at the man as if entreating him not to screw them so tight.

No further distinct recollections connected with

the scene come to my mind. I cannot now recall the state of my feelings. I know only that they were generally a mixture of horror, and pity, and admiration, and exaltation—religious views of Heaven, mixed with a detestation of Deism and Naturalism, which at such moments seemed destined to prevail over the Christian Religion in France.

The same day these four victims were immolated upon the fatal Guillotine; they were taken, I think, as was often the case, from the Tribunal[6] to the Scaffold, which stood permanently erected under the windows.

The case of Mr. Touchet, Rector of the Parish of St. Hélier, at Rennes.

The Rev. Mr. Touchet was the Rector of St. Hélier, one of the parishes in the suburbs of Rennes. During the "Terror" he was concealed in the house of the Demoiselles Ergault. There were three sisters of them, unmarried, pious, devoted women. One of them was a nun of St. Thomas of Ville-

[6] The tribunal represented in the drawing, before which M. Raoul and the sisters were tried, if we may use such an expression, was the Regular Criminal Court. There were besides, as I have mentioned, two other Tribunals of Death in our poor city of Rennes—one, the Military Commission, presided over by Morin; and the Revolutionary Tribunal, under the presidency of Brutus Magnier. Morin and Magnier were strangers to our city.—*Note by Bishop Bruté.*

neuve, at the Hospital of Vannes, but had been driven out for remaining faithful to her vows, and refusing to take the civic oaths. I often visited Mr. Touchet in his place of concealment. He was my confessor after Mr. Carron went to England. I was, of course, obliged to use great care when I went to see him, and I well remember the cautious manner of introduction; the back room where he was concealed,[7] his manner, the room itself, the curtains, and every little circumstance are indelibly impressed upon my memory. When I had finished my confession, he would often say to me that perhaps it was the last time I would have an opportunity of going to my confession to him, that perhaps that day or the next he would be discovered and led to the scaffold. When the last stretch of rage caused the Convention to put forth the law, denouncing death on those who should harbour a Priest, the good ladies felt happy at the prospect of receiving their reward by dying with Mr. Touchet, if they should be found out. Before he had heard the news they took counsel together and formed their resolution. When the horrid decree came to his knowledge, he went to them and said, "I will leave you to-night." They asked, "Where

7 The house was on the corner of the 'Rue Dauphine' and the 'Rue Châteaurenaud.' Many zealous, faithful families occupied that corner on the two streets—the Desbuillons, Rebulets, Boudons, Beauvais, Frout; the place was often subject to domiciliary visits on the part of the authorities.—*Note by Bishop Bruté.*

are you going?" "To the fields, as long as I can hide myself in the woods, and thickets, and ditches. I am resigned to die, but I will be the occasion of death to no one." But they told him that they would be but too happy to die with him; that they had unanimously taken their resolution, and made their little testamentary dispositions,[8] if any were allowed, and that, moreover, as they could only die once, whether for concealing one or many, they had sent word to some of their friends that if they were afraid of this new Law they might send to them the Priests they had concealed, and they would cheerfully receive and shelter them. The good Nun added gaily, "I have sewed into the hem of my robe a flint, a match, and a candle, so that when we are left alone in our dungeon we may have light enough to recite our Breviary[9] for the last time." It happened, however, that although they often had three Priests hidden in their house at one time, they were never discovered and apprehended, and I continued to visit Mr. Touchet there, from time to time, until the persecution was over, and he was permitted to resume the public exercise of his ministry, not at St. Hélier's,[10] however, but at St.

[8] The property of those who were put to death was confiscated. It was partly restored at a later period, but not that of those who had emigrated.

[9] The Nuns, properly so called, are obliged to recite the daily office of the Church, the same as Priests.

[10] St. Hélier was turned into a Powder-Magazine, the windows filled up with masonry, the steeple taken down, &c. St. Augustin's was turned

Augustin's, where he remained until his death, about 1806.

Mr. Massiot, the Vicar of Mr. Touchet, at St. Hélier's, was deported or banished to Cayenne, in South America, where so many died. He lived to escape, and having made his way, with incredible hardships, through the woods and morasses which lie back of the settlement, finally reached the United States. From thence he went to England, and, after the law of death was repealed, returned to France, though still exposed to prison and transportation. When the persecution had entirely ceased he was appointed Curé of Brutz, a Parish about six miles from the city, where I was sent to assist during three weeks at Easter, in 1809. He suffered very severely from rheumatism, which was the consequence of his blessed hardships during the time of the persecution.

Death of the Rev. Mr. Sorette, Professor of Humanities at the College of Rennes.

The Abbé Sorette was a young Priest, not yet thirty years of age, when he was appointed Pro-

into a Blacksmith-shop for the troops—the whole interior was lined with anvils—forges at which they shod the horses; the pavement was broken and covered with the dirt and filth of the shop, which constantly resounded with oaths and vile songs.—*Note by Bishop Bruté.*

See *Journal* for an account of the Abbé Touchet's restoration to his Parish.

fessor at the College of Rennes, the first year of the French Revolution. I studied under him, and became very much attached to him, and he took a particular interest in me, and sometimes did my mother the honour to come and dine with us. The charming modesty, candour, piety, and yet sprightliness and gaiety of that most excellent man, endeared him to all who knew him. When the Revolutionary oaths were imposed upon the Clergy, he refused to take them, and being expelled in consequence from the College, he retired to the Country Parish of Le Chatellier near Parigné,[11] 16

[11] I found among the Bishop's papers the following letter from Mr. Sorette to the Bishop's mother, written from this place. The Bishop had written upon it: "A martyr since; wounded by a ball, he was obliged to stop. They gave him five minutes to pray and then dispatched him—my good Teacher!" The letter itself gives, in its simple details, a very good idea of the manner in which "Revolutions" are brought about, and is not without instruction as bearing upon what is taking place in other parts of Europe in our days.

PARIGNE, 10 June, 1791.

MADAME,

When I arrived at Parigné, on the 3d of June, I found them all in great distress. Our dear and excellent pastor, M. Guignette, had been displaced on the 29th of May, by Dom. Verdier, Bernardine, Prior of the Abbey of Savigney. The inhabitants of Parigné were not all disposed to submit to the change and accept the person who had thus been forced upon them; they assembled in a crowd around the Presbytery, and would certainly have pelted him with sticks and stones if it had not been for their old Parish Priest, who at last succeeded in appeasing them. The intruder had only four or five persons at his High Mass, and no more at the processions on the Rogation days. One man carried the banner, another the Cross, the *Curé* sung the Litanies, and a man and two women, who were his domestics, followed and sung the "ora pro nobis." On Ascension day he was afraid to celebrate Mass, and shut himself up in the Presbytery, with some soldiers and other persons, who kept guard for eight days.

or 18 miles from Rennes. It was here that he had been stationed by the Bishop, when first ordained, and during the few years of his ministry had won

On last Sunday, a detachment of the National Militia from Fougéres entered our town about 9 o'clock in the forenoon, with arms in their hands, crying out, "To the lamp-posts with the aristocrats," and demanding the heads of all Priests who had refused to take the civic oath. I was the only Priest in the village, the Rector and Curé having fled the day previous to keep out of the way of the lamp-post, with which the mob had threatened them for a long time. Just as these troops arrived, I had left the house to go and say Mass in a private chapel, but they had nailed up the door, and declared that if they caught me they would cut off my head.

These soldiers rung the bell for High Mass and Vespers; they forced a number of persons to enter the Church, and shut others up in a Press House, which they called their Guard House (corps de garde). They also assembled the Municipality by force, and compelled about twenty or thirty persons to certify the *installation of M. Verdier, Curé.* They, in fact, entered upon the register the names of several persons who did not sign; others signed it through fear, surrounded by bayonets, and with the intention of withdrawing their adhesion the first opportunity that presented itself.

One of the soldiers mounted up by a ladder, which was placed against the wall inside of the Church, to efface some armorial bearings; but finding himself slipping, he caught hold of a statue of St. Michael, to save himself, but the statue, not being very firm on its base, both he and the statue came tumbling down together.

At last, about 6 o'clock in the evening, they beat the retreat and started for home, having left with M. the Rector a note, without signature, ordering all refractory Priests to leave the Parish within twenty-four hours, under pain of being strung up to the lamp-post.

During the eight days which are now passed since the Rector and Curé left, I have found myself so lonely that it seems as if I had been cast all at once into a desert place. You see scarcely any one moving about—our good people remain in concealment. In vain do the bells ring out, to call them to the church; the sound is no longer a source of pleasure to them, but of grief, and causes them to shed tears of regret and bitterness. We are obliged to go six or seven miles to be present at Mass. Those who are in favour of the present order of things watch my every word and action, in order to find an excuse for driving me out the Parish. I am, indeed,

the unbounded affection of his own and all the neighbouring Parishes. "Mr. Sorette!" with what an accent of affection was that name pronounced by every one, before his death and many years afterwards. At Le Chatellier he exercised the duties of his holy ministry, during the worst times of the Revolution, with an undaunted zeal, surrounded in the vicinity by many other Priests of the same fearless, unreserved devotedness; some of whom were at last, like himself, amongst the victims which the Diocese of Rennes offered to God for the cruel sins and horrid excesses of the times.

He indeed escaped during the whole reign of Robespierre, and until the laws of death were repealed. Banishment to French Guiana for the younger Priests, perpetual imprisonment for the older ones, who should exercise any of the func-

in a sad condition, but I do not wish to leave my mother until matters are in a better state. The new Parish Priests are not acceptable to the people in our district. At Fougéres, as here, the people will not go to their Mass. Their few partisans, however, are very zealous in their favour, and it has already caused much disturbance and bad feeling. I am told that in some cases they have turned their servants, and even their relatives, out of doors, because they refused to be present at Mass, when celebrated by the intruders. I did not have the satisfaction of seeing my dear friend the Abbé of Chateaugiron, in my journey from Rennes. When you have an opportunity please give him news of me, and to my Gabriel, to whom I wish all success in his studies.

If possible, I would wish to have a place of refuge prepared for me, to which I may escape, if proscribed a second time, as they constantly threaten me at Fougéres.

I have the honour, madame, to remain, with profound respect and sincere gratitude, your humble and obedient servant,

SORETTE, Priest.

tions of the holy ministry, were the milder orders of the day.

The more zealous Jacobins, however, were much displeased at this relaxation of the law, and often eluded it. When they discovered any Priests in the country, and were not restrained by the presence of some magistrate or leader not so desperately bent on the destruction of the Priests as themselves, they would often deliberately put them to death on the spot, rather than bring them to the city and deliver them up to the authorities.

This was the fate of my dear and respected Professor. Unfortunately for him, the part of the Department where he lived had always been most active and conspicuous in its opposition to the National Convention, so generally manifested in the West, on both sides of the River Loire.

The position of the Priests there was exceedingly painful. Naturally, and from principle, inclined to the side of the opposition, their sacred character hindered them from mixing in the horrors of civil war. They simply continued to fulfil the functions of their holy ministry wherever they could, ready to carry the succors of religion to whoever asked for them, whether friend or foe.[12] In consequence, it

[12] "It has been falsely asserted," says the Marchioness de la Rochejaquelein, "that the Priests fought, but they came to the field of battle only to confess the dying, which they did in the hottest fire; and it is true that their bodies were occasionally found. . . . They have been reproached also with having excited the Vendeans to cruelty. Nothing could be more

often happened that they were obliged to be present, and prepare for death those who fell victims to the severe, and sometimes unjustifiable, measures by which the insurgents retaliated the cruelties of those who were called the patriots. A Priest could not, of course, refuse his ministry even under such circumstances, and if he could not persuade the infuriated leaders or agents of the insurrection to spare the lives of their enemies, he was obliged, nevertheless, to be present, and try to save their souls. It will readily be perceived that the exercise of their ministry under such circumstances offered but too good a ground, especially in such excited times, for the horrid calumny that the Priests excited and urged on the people to these cruel deeds of retaliation and revenge. It cannot be doubted that these stories animated the enemies and persecutors of the clergy to persevere in the schemes which had been laid under Robespierre for their utter extermination, and which they now saw to a certain extent foiled by the relaxation in the law.

false; and, on the contrary, I could produce many traits of courageous humanity highly honourable to them. Numbers owed their lives to their intercessions with furious soldiers bent on slaughter. M. Douissis, Curé of Saint Marié de Rhé, a most ardent follower of the army, prevented the massacre of a great number of prisoners, by his feeling and eloquent exhortations. Some years afterwards, being brought before a Republican Tribunal, this action saved him."—*Memoirs of the Marchioness de la Rochejaquelein*, p. 236–7.

Mr. Sorette led a life of continual alarm and danger, yet of untiring zeal in the fulfilment of his duties. All his labours, however, I am certain, were strictly kept within the pure and perfect line of his priestly functions, which so excellent a man would have cherished more dearly than his existence. To be finally spent by the sacrifice of his life, after so hard and faithful a service, during his many years of concealment in his own Parish and the neighbouring parts, was to him an enviable conclusion of his work. Such were the sentiments he expressed to me, with much fervour and alacrity of mind, two or three weeks before his death.

He had at that time come to our city on his way to the mineral waters of Guichen, twelve miles further to the south. He had been advised to go there for a double purpose—to repair his health, which was much shattered by labour and exposure, and to escape for a while from the search made for his apprehension in his own part of the country with redoubled activity. He was concealed in the suburb St. Martin (à la Pechardière en St. Grégoire) at the château of the Ladies De Leon, and whilst there sent word to my mother to let me come and see him. My mother gave me the most earnest charge to persuade him not to venture to Guichen, but to come to our house and be secreted, where he could be nursed and well taken care of, the better because several physicians, good, religious men, were in the habit of visiting our family. I hurried to him with most pleasing hopes to have under our roof my beloved preceptor—and so good a Priest—but they were in vain! I arrived at the place, La Pechardière, was very cautiously admitted, and enjoyed a most agreeable interview with him. He related to me many of his wonderful escapes. But when I had easily made out to prove to him that it would be very unsafe for him to take up his residence near the waters of Guichen, the conclusion he drew was, that he had already yielded too much to the advice of the physicians, that he was not so ill as they thought, and that the best thing he could do was to return to his poor people, and remain with them to the last. No arguments, no entreaties, could make him accede to the wishes of his friends at Rennes. Two or three days afterwards he returned to Parigné, or Le Chatellier. I never heard directly from him again, though he was accustomed, from time to time, to write to me during those dreadful days which were now drawing to a close for him.

About three weeks after he had returned to his mission we received the following information in regard to his end. I remember and relate almost the words in which the tale was told to me: Poor Mr. Sorette was called the other day to administer the last sacrament to an old woman in a little farm house. He had finished, and was coming back to his hiding place, when a party of Contre-Chouans,[13] who were patrolling the country in search of victims, and who knew that Mr. Sorette was concealed somewhere in that vicinity, asked a peasant girl whom they met if she could tell them where they would find the Priest, as they needed his services for a sick person. It so happened that she had met Mr. Sorette but a few moments before, and deceived by their disguise, and supposing them to be friends, she said to them, after a moment's hesitation, Mr. Sorette has left that house yonder but a minute since, and is passing along the hedge there by the meadow. They immediately ran after him, and as soon as they drew near fired their guns at him and broke his arm. He immediately stopped and surrendered, and then told them to lead him to the city. But they knowing that in such a case he would be only exiled to Cayenne, told him that they had resolved to put him to death. Mr. Sorette then entreated them to allow him a few minutes to say his prayers and prepare himself for death. He then knelt down on the grass, and, when they had waited a few moments, they shot him on the spot. Some of his murderers were known, and among them two or three rabid Jacobins, who had committed many crimes of a similar

[13] *Patriots*, as they called themselves, in the disguise of Chouans, the name given to those in that part of Brittany who had risen up against the Revolutionary Government.

character during the time of Robespierre and afterwards. Among the Parishioners of Mr. Sorette, some were found more ready to obey the feeling of indignation and revenge excited by his death than those of mercy and forgiveness, which he had so constantly preached to them when alive. These watched their opportunity, and, to complete the picture of those sad times, we heard soon afterwards that some of his murderers had been killed, and sent to meet their holy victim before the Judgment seat. Alas! they were more to be pitied than he—he, in truth, so exceedingly happy. At the altar, that morning, in some hidden corner, the holy communion received as viaticum, his ministry of consolation and grace to the poor dying woman, and then kneeling quietly on the grass, probably his last words of prayer, like St. Stephen's, offered up for those blind men, and his life a holocaust of peace for his unhappy country.

Death of the Rev. Mr. Duval, Rector of Laignelet.

I was present when Mr. Duval, who was a very respectable Physician at Rennes, received the news of the murder of his elder brother, the Abbé Duval, Rector of Laignelet, a Parish in the country, near Mr. Sorette's, about 18 miles from Rennes.

I had only seen the Abbé Duval once or twice at

his brother's in Rennes. He was about 40 or 45 years of age, a very mild and serene countenance, meekness being, indeed, a particular characteristic of his disposition.

He had persevered throughout the whole time of the persecution to exercise his holy ministry with unabated zeal—no less devoted to his good people that they were attached to him, and they were exceedingly so.

It became known, by some means or other, to the bloodthirsty hounds who were continually searching after the Priests, that Mr. Duval was to go, on a certain night, to baptize the child of some poor peasants who lived in a little cabin in the woods on the confines of his Parish, and they, consequently, placed themselves in ambuscade near the way by which they knew he would pass. He started late in the evening with his guide, and had approached so near to his intended murderers before he saw them that there was no chance for him to make his escape. He said to the man that was with him that their only course was to advance boldly towards them, and that, perhaps, that very boldness might deceive them. The man hung back, but the Priest walked steadily on his way as if apprehending no danger. No sooner, however, had he come opposite to the place where his enemies stood, than one of them crossed the road towards him and, lifting up Mr. Duval's hat, said to him, "Is it thou,

Duval?" and the others who had followed him, placing their guns against his breast, shot him dead upon the spot. The guide, who stood near, fled at that moment, and could give no further particulars—except those which I have related. The poor parents of the child he was to baptize heard the report of the guns, but dared not venture out immediately. When they thought that the murderers had retired, they went in the dead of the night, and, with the assistance of some neighbours, rendered the last and only tokens of respect in their power to the body of their beloved pastor, by burying it near the place where he had been murdered. Oh! how the horrors of those times rush in upon my recollections when I write these things.

A Priest and Peasant bound together and led to the "Fusillade," singing the Service for the Dead.

One morning I was seated early at my studies, about half-past five o'clock, when, to my surprise, I heard at a distance the notes of the "Libera me Domine" from the burial service of the church sung by some one in the streets. The singers were evidently hurrying along fast, and the sounds grew more and more clear and distinct as they approached the square upon which our house stood. For two years all such chants had ceased in our streets, and therefore I jumped up and ran hastily to the window to see from whom they proceeded. I immediately perceived a group of twenty or thirty soldiers hurrying along two men bound together, both in the garb of peasants, but I saw immediately that one of them was a Priest; his black hair floating upon his shoulders, his beard long unshaven, the very hat upon his head, are present to my vivid recollections.

I understood too well what it all meant, and ran to the door to go out and follow them, agitated and partially frightened with the usual terror which rested on my heart, but at the same time animated by the song of death, for it was the Priest who was thus singing his own *Libera*, and the poor peasant stepped along quickly by his side, looking, as may be supposed, very serious, but without the least appearance of fear. The impression on my mind is that the soldiers, who generally followed their prisoners with jokes and abuse, accompanied these two in silence.

I crossed the square, following close upon their footsteps. At the turn of the street the good Priest had finished the *Libera*, and commenced singing the *Miserere*. The peasant, if I remember rightly, was also busy at his prayers, but I do not recollect the appearance of his countenance as distinctly as that of the priest, who was apparently about 50 years of age, of middling stature, and who was dressed, as I have said, in the short, coarse, brown coat of the peasants.

They moved along with great rapidity, so much so that, although I left them at the end of the street, when they had but one short street to pass through to reach the public walk, where I dared not follow them and be present, I had hardly reached our house when I heard the report of the guns simultaneously, as if but one, and their victims were in eternity. I immediately entered the house, and hastened to relate what I seen to my mother, and her friend Mademoiselle Chateaugiron, who was with her. My mother immediately said, "We know it all; we were praying for them." I remember my mother's look at that moment—such a mingled look of sorrow and firmness—and that immediately afterwards all the family went about their ordinary family affairs, as if nothing particular had happened; and so it was, for death was a daily tale.

The only circumstance at all peculiar in this case was their permitting him to sing the office for the dead as he hurried along, and the early hour at which the execution took place. It may be that they had been tried late at night, and the commanding officer wished, for some reason or other, to deprive the public of their usual little excitement, or, what is more probable, was utterly indifferent about it, and thought it just as well to dispatch them at that early hour as at a more busy time of the day.

I do not remember the name of the victim in this case. It seems to me that it was Boutier,[14] or some similar name

---

Rev. Mr. Tostivint, and the Marquis and Marchioness de Bedée.

The Marquis De Bedée resided, with the Marchioness his wife, at his château on the rich and beautiful estate of Bedée, about four leagues from Rennes. They were both advanced in age (between 60 and 70) and had been married over forty years.

The Rev. Mr. Tostivint,[15] the chaplain and tutor

[14] The Abbé Tresvaux, "History of the Persecution in Brittany," (vol. ii. p. 21,) in his account of the martyrdom of M. Matthieu Louis Bouttier, Vicar of Mézières, in the Diocese of Rennes, mentions that on his way to the place of execution he chanted the Litany of the Blessed Virgin, and the Burial Office of the Church. The authorities had arrested his brother, and declared that they would not let him go unless the Priest gave himself up, which, from fraternal affection, he did, and they immediately put them both to death.

[15] His name (Carron, vol. ii. p. 501) was John Baptiste Tostivint, a native of Landujan, in the Diocese of St. Malo, Vicar of the Parish of Evran, in the same Diocese ; he was guillotined at Rennes, 26th July, 1794. He had been Chaplain to M. de Bedée, immediately after his ordination for three years, at the end of which time he was appointed by Monseigneur Laurens, the Bishop of St. Malo, Vicar of the Parish of Evran, and he had served that Parish 10 years when the Revolution broke out. He manifested the greatest devotion to his duties in confirming all over whom he had any influence in their attachment to the Faith. Having refused to take the oath of adhesion to the civil constitution of the Clergy, he was exposed to severe persecution, and, at length, forced to take refuge in the Island of Jersey in Sept., 1792. He remained there, however, only about two

to the family, was discovered by the Revolutionary agents concealed in a small building or garden house, in no manner connected with the castle, and in which any fugitive might have taken refuge without the knowledge of the family.

The Marquis and Marchioness were, however, arrested at the same time with the Priest, and brought before the Revolutionary Tribunal. The

months and a half, when, on account of the violence of the persecution, the number of Priests that were put to death, and the consequent need of those who remained faithful to their religion, he, like many others, would not remain in security any longer, but returned to France, to afford all the succor that was in his power. The first time that he attempted to return he was driven back by a storm, but about a fortnight after, having found another opportunity, he embarked again and reached the coast of France. From this moment until arrested he was never idle; his labors were not confined to his Parish, but he wandered about in disguise amongst the neighbouring Parishes, hearing confessions and administering to the sick. He had been seen to administer the sacrament to a sick person, when about 10 o'clock in the evening he arrived at the château of M. de Bedée, to hear confessions. After having finished, he retired to the garden house to spend the rest of the night. He had been watched, however, and was denounced to the authorities. M. de Bedée hearing the noise made by the gensdarmes, jumped out of the window to give warning to the Priest. They were both arrested, as related above, and a few days afterwards Madame Bedée.

Father Carron does not mention the scene before the tribunal, but gives an extract from a letter which M. de Bedée wrote to his son before his death, in which he exhorts him to be faithful to his religion. "When you receive this letter you will have neither father, nor mother, nor tutor. They will take your property also. The grace of God will remain with you. Be faithful to it."

When they approached the guillotine, M. Tostivint mounted first, before M. Chilon, a Priest of Romillé, and M. and Madame Bedée; but perceiving the agitation of these last at the sight of the instrument of death, he requested permission to die last, and having consoled and assisted his friends in their death, he gently submitted to his fate. He was 39 years of age.

Priest was, of course, immediately condemned to death. The Marquis, on being questioned, naturally remarked that the hut or shed in which Mr. Tostivint had been found was open to any one who saw fit to enter it, and the Priest being there did not bring them within the provisions of the law against those who gave asylum to ecclesiastics.

But such pleas were of no avail in those times. The Marquis and his wife belonged to an ancient and noble family, and as such were obnoxious to those in power. They were, accordingly, condemned to suffer death at the same time with the Priest.

As soon as the sentence was pronounced, M. de Bedée turned toward the Marchioness and said to her, in a quiet, dignified tone of voice, "We have lived happily together forty years, madam, and it is the will of God that we should not be separated now." Madame de Bedée was seen and heard immediately to give a ready and courageous assent. The words I do not remember, nor was I present when M. de Bedée thus spoke to her, but I heard the whole scene described immediately after it took place, as most striking and affecting, particularly, they said, on account of the simple but at the same time noble and generous manner with which the Marquis, who was a person of truly dignified manner, addressed the Marchioness before the very tribunal.

The Rev. Mr. Tostivint was hardly forty years of age. I had his nephew in my class of theology when I taught in the Seminary of Rennes. I regret that I have not more particulars in regard to him—"My good Uncle," as the young man always called him, speaking to me about his death. Oh! how happy that "good Uncle" was, as I used to think when we spoke of him, thus to die for his religion.

Rev. Mr. Sacquet, Rector of St. Martin, at Rennes.

The Rev. Mr. Sacquet, Rector of St. Martin, one of the Parishes of Rennes, was of a tall stature, with a countenance full of dignity and benevolence. He was at this time about 55 years of age, and having been for many years the faithful Rector of one of the most populous parishes of the city, consisting of from two to three thousand of the poorest inhabitants in the suburb of the same name,[16] (St. Martin,) he had long enjoyed the love and veneration of his Parishioners, and the esteem of the whole city.

At the outbreak of the Revolution, Mr. Sacquet had refused to take the oaths, and I think had been exiled to England, from whence he returned and

[16] I am not sure of the extent of his Parish, between those of St. John, St. Stephen, and St. Lawrence.

lived in concealment in that part of the country which was nearest to his Parish, or rather within its precincts, for, as was known at my mother's, his usual hiding place was in a spot near the last house of the suburb. Late one evening a report reached our house that "Mr. Sacquet had been denounced, and that they were making strict search for his person in the suburb and adjoining parts." Of course, all of us were in the greatest anxiety, and passed a sleepless night in lamentations over those dreadful times and fervent prayers for his escape, the frequent and usual occupation of such hours during those days and nights of misery. The least noise in the street startled us. I remember, however, there were often mixed with these natural fears and regrets a sense and expressions of his happiness if he was taken, in thus suffering for his religion—sometimes ejaculations: "Oh! my Lord, if they cannot find him." "Oh! if you would be pleased to spare him to us." "Alas! our country is too much disgraced by such a deluge of crimes." "All religion will soon be taken from us." But morning came, and the first news was "*He is taken.*" At 4 o'clock, early this morning, did they find him in a field of wheat which they had completely surrounded, and then searching diligently every part, they found him. He has, of course, refused to name the person who had previously given him an asylum, having chosen to go out into the open fields rather than to remain hidden in the house which was denounced yesterday, and which he left as soon as he was told that the persecutors were coming.

He was brought before the tribunal in the afternoon of the same day, and had a very short interrogatory to undergo—only sufficient to identify his person, which, besides, was familiarly known to every one in the city, and to none better than to the Judges on the Bench. I was present at the examination, but do not remember any particular question or answer. His whole appearance, however—his features, the expression of his countenance, such an indescribable mixture of dignity and self-possession, and mildness—is as present to me at this moment as it was then. I can hear the sound of his voice now, as, slowly, calmly, and with a certain quiet self-possession, he gave the short answers which the questions required. I remember that all present were impressed by the scene, and there was much more decorum than usual, both in the tribunal and amongst the spectators. Neither can I recall the charge and sentence of the Judge; my impression is, that his words and manner were softened by the common influence of that countenance, of which so many said afterwards "it seemed as if it was our Lord during His passion," and others, "he was like a lamb before so many ravening wolves."

After the sentence of death had been passed, it was found that the executioner, contrary to his usual custom, was absent. They were obliged to wait half an hour or more before he came, and then, with great brutality and affected hurry, he began to strip the venerable confessor and prepare him immediately for the scaffold, rudely cutting off his hair and cutting away the collar of his shirt, to leave his neck bare for the axe, tying his hands behind his back, and then throwing his coat loosely over his shoulders. I saw him passing along the corridors of the Court House (Palais de Justice) on his way to the guillotine, which was but two hundred steps off; his person was tall, of rather a full habit and very strong constitution. The cruel executioner, in so hastily preparing him for the scaffold, had wounded him in the neck, and the blood was running down his breast, but as he passed along to the place of execution no other words could so well express his tranquillity and composure than by saying that he looked at that moment as he used to look when following the processions of the people of his Parish, on the solemn festivals of the Church. But though I followed him so near, I dared not go and witness the exact moment of his blessed departure from such a world of sin and misery.[17]

[17] M. Carron, vol. iii. p. 203, gives an account of the life and martyrdom of Mr. Sacquet. His Christian name was Francis Julien, born in the

The Rev. Mr. Poirier, the Rev. Mr. Emery, and four other Priests put to death at Rennes in 1796.

One day five Priests were tried and sentenced, and executed together.[18] I remember the names of only two of them, Mr. Emery and Mr. Poirier. I was acquainted with Mr. Emery, a small, thin man, but strong and energetic in heart and mind. When the persecution was most severe, and many were being sacrificed to its fury, he never relaxed

Parish of All Saints, at Rennes, 22d Aug., 1730. He enjoyed a high reputation, not only on account of his eminent virtues, but as a most instructive and touching Preacher. He was naturally of a timid disposition, but Grace gave him strength and fortitude. When the law of deportation was passed, he hid himself, as related above, within the precincts of his parish, and continued to afford the consolations of religion to his people until arrested. The name of the person who concealed him was John Lemée, a peasant. M. Carron relates that during his trial and execution he manifested the greatest composure and fortitude, and as he placed his head under the fatal axe he repeated one of the verses of the Ps. *Miserere*—Benigne fac Domine, etc. "Deal favourably, O Lord, in thy good will with Sion, that the walls of Jerusalem may be built up." He was put to death 14th Aug., 1794.

18 According to Tresvaux, vol. ii. p. 24, there were but four executed at this time: the two mentioned in the text; Mr. Gautier, Vicaire of Bruc, in the Diocese of St. Malo, of whose arrest and death so interesting an account is given hereafter, and Mr. Crosson, of the Diocese of Rennes. Mr. Emery was a native of La Chapelle Bouéxie, where Bp. Bruté's sister resided, and where he met him as mentioned in the narrative. He intoned the *Te Deum* on mounting the scaffold. They were put to death on the day of a Fair, and in the midst of the assemblage; but the country people left the place. M. Poirier belonged to one of the most respectable and wealthy families of Miniac-sous-Bécherel. The National Guard who arrested him were disposed to let him go, but they were dissuaded by an inhabitant of his native place, who was among them. M. Poirier's last injunctions to his family at Bécherel were to pardon the man who had been the cause of his arrest and death.

his zeal. It was natural that one so devoted to his religion and king should sympathize with the reaction produced by the revolutionary cruelties, and it was said that he was seen with those who had taken up arms to resist the Revolution. I remember seeing his name mentioned in the proclamations, posted up at the corners of the streets by the authority of the Representative who then ruled over us, or rather, trampled on us, in the name of the Convention and the General commanding the troops. The enemies of the clergy, of course, took advantage of their presence with the Insurgents, and particularly of their administering the sacraments to those whom they put to death, to represent them as aiding and abetting in these cruelties. But however much they disapproved of the "lex talionis" which the Chouans were, we may say, driven to put in practice, they could not refuse their ministry to those who became its victims. Mr. Emery was, no doubt, an active partisan in rousing and keeping alive a spirit of resistance to the revolutionary government. He was known often to celebrate Mass for them in the fields, upon the elevated spots of the "landes," as they are called in Brittany, vast, uncultivated, wild parts of the country, resembling in appearance the wild prairies of the West. Often five and six thousand persons and more would assemble together, with outposts and watchful friends at a distance, to give the alarm in case of any approaching danger from the Republicans, or Blues, as they were called. A short time before he was arrested I was on a visit to my sister, at La Chapelle Bouéxie, about 20 miles from Rennes, a very wild and romantic part of the country, and having accompanied her husband, who went out shooting, we suddenly came, on turning a corner of the road, upon three men dressed as peasants, and on accosting them we discovered that it was Mr. Emery and two other Priests. My brother-in-law expostulated with Mr. Emery and his companions very strongly on their imprudence in thus exposing themselves in the open day. The remotest Parishes were no safer at that time than those near to the cities; the whole country swarmed with Gendarmes, spies, and Contre-Chouans, as they were called—that is, persons who dressed themselves like the Insurgents, the better to discover them. It is impossible now to conceive of the earnestness with which they hunted after denounced persons, and especially the Priests. At that time the law of death within twenty-four hours was still in force.

A few days after this meeting, Mr. Emery and five other Priests were arrested and brought together before the "Criminal Court"[19] at Rennes. My mother saw them as they passed under our

[19] Not the "Revolutionary Tribunal." The persecution of the Priests at that time came within the jurisdiction of the ordinary courts.

windows, on their way to the Tribunal. She was struck, she said, by the remarkable appearance of Mr. Poirier, a tall old man, with grey hair and most dignified and heavenly countenance, and at that moment she witnessed a circumstance which will give, better than any long description, an idea of the spirit of the times.

The Guillotine at Rennes, as in most other cities, stood permanently erected upon the public square, quite bloody, and sometimes with heads exposed upon it. The Gendarmes, as they passed along with their prisoners on their way to the Tribunal, were accustomed to call their attention to it, and make them look at the fatal scaffold which they were so soon to ascend. "Look there," said one of them to Mr. Poirier on this occasion, "take a look at Madame Guillotine;"[20] the mob at the same time crying out, as usual, "To the Guillotine with them!" The venerable old man seemed to take no notice of what he said, and did not turn his face towards it, but walked along modestly with the others. The Gendarme, offended, no doubt, at his composure and disregard of his order, immediately struck him a severe blow in the face, saying, "Will you not look there when I tell you? You will soon be there yourself." "I see it," answered

[20] The Guillotine afforded a constant subject for jests and ribaldry; it was called "Madame" and other names. A person who was about to be executed was said to be about "to marry Madame Guillotine," &c.

Mr. Poirier, quietly. These words were related to me by others who were near, and overheard them, but the *blow* dwelt in my mother's memory, and years afterwards, when speaking of those dreadful scenes, she would often mention it. "Of all those whom I saw passing to the Tribunal, and from thence to the scaffold, none had a more venerable appearance than Mr. Poirier," and then she would tell of that shameful act of barbarity, which, however, was no doubt to Mr. Poirier a precious trait of resemblance to our Lord in his own passion. I do not now recall to mind any peculiar circumstance in their judgment, except this one, so much in character of the fearless and energetic Mr. Emery. The President of the Tribunal, Bouassier, had been his school-mate, and was in the same class with him at College. When, after the usual formal interrogatories, he passed the sentence of death upon his old friend, and the venerable men who shared his fate, Mr. Emery immediately addressed him in Latin, reproaching him and those whose cause he served with their crimes, and reminding him of the Tribunal of an outraged God, before which he would one day have to appear. The Judge turned pale and appeared much agitated, but called upon the Gendarmes to silence him.

They were guillotined, the five of them together, the same day.

The Rector of Guignen and his Vicar.

The Rector of Guignen,[21] a venerable old man, and his Vicar, had been a short time before guillotined in the city of Rennes, when I went to see my sister, Madame Junsions, who lived at "La Chapelle Bouéxie," a short distance from Guignen; and she then related to me the following incidents of the capture of these two victims:

They had been warned of the search that was being made for them, and attempted to escape through the fields, when they were perceived by those in pursuit of them. They were, however, a considerable distance ahead, and the Vicar, who was much the youngest and more active, might easily have escaped. They gained, however, upon the old Priest, firing their guns at him as they pursued him. The Vicar had crossed a brook and ascended the opposite bank, and was out of the reach of his pursuers, when, looking back, he perceived that the aged Rector was unable to get up the steep ascent. His pursuers were shouting with joy at his unavailing efforts. The young man immediately turned back, to the surprise of the soldiers, who could not but admire his heroic charity, and endeavoured to assist the good old Parish Priest. He descended the bank, recrossed the brook, and,

[21] Am not certain in regard to the Parish, whether Guipry, Guichen, or Guignen, but the facts were as here related.—*Note by Bp. Bruté.*

covering him with his body, strove to aid him across. But he was unable to do so before the soldiers came up and took them prisoners, to be led, as both knew well, to certain death. The Gendarmes stopped at my sister's house with their prisoners on their way to the city. The leader of the party, the infamous and dreaded D——n, who had already distinguished himself by many similar captures, and was a man of frightful aspect and most sanguinary disposition, told my sister the circumstances which I have related above, with some expressions of a sort of admiration and pity, the more striking from the mouth of such a monster. "I almost regret," he said, "that such a brave fellow will have to be put to death after such a noble action. He was quite safe, citizeness (citoyenne)," he added. "We had given him up, but we were gaining on the old one, when lo! he turned back and came to help him cross the brook, and all the time he kept covering the old man with his body against the fire of our guns. It was a remarkable and affecting scene." Yet as soon as they had got some refreshments they hurried on with their prisoners to the Tribunal, and from the Tribunal they went, the same day, to the scaffold.

f 154

The Rev. Mr. Clement, the Rev. Mr. Casson, the Rev. Mr. Rangervé.

The Rev. Mr. Clement[22] was the name of a good old Priest who remained concealed in Rennes during the worst of the persecution, venturing out in disguise, however, often at night, to visit the sick and others who needed him. One night he was obliged to pass near the box of one of the sentries, who hailed him with the usual "Qui vive," "Who goes there?" If he had returned immediately and resolutely the usual answer, "Citizen," he would, in all probability, have been allowed to pass by unmolested, but a sort of ill-judged and ill-timed scruple seized him, as he related afterwards when in prison, and he hesitated to answer by a word which, in the sense they used it in those times as designating one who was friendly to the present order of things, seemed to him to be a lie. He, therefore, made a vague answer, and attempted to

[22] M. René Clement, according to Tresvaux, vol. ii. p. 19, was a native of Rennes, and Vicaire of Brielles. At the time that Le Coz, the Constitutional Bishop, took possession of Rennes, Monseigneur De Goiac having been driven into exile, he published a pastoral letter, which the Mayor of Brielles obliged M. Clement to read from the pulpit. He did so, but at the same time made a running commentary upon it, pointing out the opposition between its principles and those of the Catholic Church. For this he was fined and imprisoned. While imprisoned he published a pamphlet, in which, with great talent and sharpness, he refuted the sophistries of the intruded Bishop. Having escaped from prison, he went to Rennes. Each week he made a tour in the surrounding country, visiting the sick, administering the sacraments, &c. He was put to death on the 5th of April, 1794, aged about 30 years.

escape by running, thus immediately revealing his suspicious character. He was, of course, immediately pursued and arrested, and soon after put to death. I remember no other particulars in regard to him, except that he enjoyed an excellent character and was very much respected, and long after those sad days "poor Mr. Clement," or "that worthy Mr. Clement," was often heard uttered with much feeling by the lips of those who had known him

The Rev. Mr. Casson was arrested at the house of Madame Le Grand, an elderly lady of our city of great piety and zeal. By his presence of mind, however, that excellent man saved his protectress from sharing his fate. Being informed that the Gendarmes were coming to search for him, he would not, notwithstanding her entreaties, remain in the place of concealment which had been prepared for him, but went down stairs and stood behind the door, which was the common entrance of all those who, according to the French custom, had their apartments in the different stories of the house, only one of which was occupied by Madame Le Grand. It was remarkable, however, that she escaped even in this manner; for her attachment to religion was well known, and the information was most positive that Mr. Casson was concealed in the apartments of this good lady. I was told that she regretted very much not having been permitted to leave this world by so happy a death, and I can easily believe it from my remembrance of the dispositions and feelings of fervent Catholics in those times.

The Rev. Mr. Rangervé[23] was the Rector of St. Saviour's, one of the Parishes of Rennes. He was arrested in the country about 35 miles from Rennes, in company with two brothers La Bigotière, and a Mr. Du Plessis of the Royal army. Mr. Du Plessis had his thigh broken by a bullet, and was carried to the Tribunal seated in a chair. They were all condemned to death. The Abbé Rangervé was a man of very commanding appearance and polished manner. At his trial he seemed to

[23] It appears from Mr. Carron's account, vol. i. p. 551, that the family name was Rolland, and that the name by which he was known and mentioned in the above sketch was taken, according to the customs of those times, from a Seigniory belonging to his family. He was born in the Château of Roches-Martinois, within the limits of the Diocese of St. Malo, on the 9th of July, 1756. He made his studies in the College of Rennes, and when ordained Priest was first Vicaire in the Parishes of All Saints, and afterwards in St. Hélier's, and finally in St. Saviour's. When the Revolution broke out he took refuge in the Island of Jersey. He afterwards returned to France, in company with several gentlemen of Brittany, Messieurs de la Tremouille, De la Bigotière, Du Plessis, and was arrested at the Château of la Bigotière, having been denounced by the Farmer who superintended the Estate. Mr. Carron makes no mention of the circumstances related by Bp. Bruté, but says that a friend endeavoured to save him by declaring before the Tribunal that he had taken the "civil oath," as it was called. When, however, the Judge asked the Abbé Rangervé if this was so, he answered that it was not, that he had "never taken it, and never would." They circulated a report, he adds, which does not take away from the value of his sacrifice, but which, in reality, increases it, that he was unconscious at the moment of his death. He was guillotined with MM. De la Bigotière and M. Du Plessis, the 18th Dec., 1793.

hope that he would be spared, and gave evidence that he was much attached to life, making explanations and apologies which were strikingly in contrast with the spirit usually exhibited by his brother Priests. Nothing could be more edifying, more worthy of their holy office than their modest courage, calm resignation, and perfect serenity, made the more impressive by the turbulent and brutal conduct of their persecutors.

But in Mr. Rangervé's case, I remember, we were disappointed at what seemed a degree of weakness—accustomed as we were to see the victims act as if they felt it to be an honour to suffer in so great and glorious a cause as that of Religion—and consequently like the Indians and Iroquois, in regard to their braves, to expect that every one called to the honour of dying for his Faith would behave in every respect worthy of his exalted principles, his ancestors, the martyrs of old, and his Brethren who had already been called upon, or who would be called upon, to make "the same good confession."

Poor Mr. Rangervé did not, however, in any manner betray his duty to his God, except by this degree of weakness and natural anxiety for life. When condemned he resumed all his composure, and manifested, as I was told, on the scaffold the same firmness and dignity of bearing which graced so uniformly his brethren through the whole trial.

The Death of Rev. Mr. Le Moine, Priest of the Diocese of St. Malo.

The Rev. Mr. Le Moine was a very respectable and pious Priest, who exercised the holy ministry in the Parishes of Maure and La Chapelle Bouéxie, which last place was, as I have already stated, the residence of one of my Sisters. She went to confession to him, and when it was possible assisted at the Holy Sacrifice, at the Farm Houses in the remoter parts of the country. I often heard her speak of him as a very holy man, who preserved in the midst of all the horrors and confusion of those days a most calm and recollected mind. His death was accompanied with many atrocities. The circumstances were as follows, though stated only in substance; she could not, after all her inquiries, obtain any fuller details.

Having been arrested by a party of the Revolutionists who were scouring that part of the country, they at first intended to take him a prisoner to Rennes. When, however, they had gone four or five miles on the way, and were passing along the levée or dike which confines the waters of a large pond, or lake, near the beautiful country seat of La Masse, in the Parish of Baulon, some of the soldiers suggested that it would be better to dispatch him at once. A few of them were opposed to shedding his blood with their own hands. The more ferocious, however, prevailed, and they began to hack him to pieces with their sabres, some at the same time piercing him with their bayonets, so that he was soon dead.

These were all the circumstances I remember of which my Sister told me at the time, bewailing with a flood of tears the fate of her good Pastor. "Oh! my Brother,[24] what an excellent man Mr. Le Moine was," I remember she said.

I was in Rennes at the time this murder occurred, and we heard of it a few days after when the party of Soldiers returned to the city. I happened to hear one of them, myself, expressing his regret at what had occurred, though he was one of those

[24] I am inclined to think from the detailed relation of Tresvaux, vol. 1. p. 447, that Bishop Bruté has confounded Mr. Le Moine, Vicaire of Concale, with Mr. Barré, Priest at Mause. They both belonged to the same Diocese, and were arrested at the same time at La Chapelle Bouéxie. Having been warned of the approach of the soldiers, they fled to the woods, but Mr. Le Moine, who had been wounded in the shoulder by a ball, was obliged to stop. Mr. Barré might have escaped, but would not desert his wounded friend. They were conducted by the Gendarmes in different directions. According to Mr. Tresvaux, those who had charge of Mr. Le Moine arrested a man named Morrin, who lived near the Château de la Mace, and having found a Catechism and Rosary in his possession, which in those days were as good as a death-warrant, they led them both into the woods called the "Bois de la Grande-Fontaine," and digging a hole, they shot them on the spot, and buried them in it. A man who met the party, in charge of Mr. Barré, told the Gendarmes that he was a Farmer in his vicinity, but when they appealed to Mr. Barré to know if it was so, he would not tell a lie to save his life, but openly declared that he was a Priest. He was hacked to pieces by the Soldiers, literally piecemeal, with the most revolting cruelty, and they afterwards carried parts of his body through the town on the points of their bayonets.

who had been maddened by the errors of those times to an excess of rage against everything holy and good which it is almost impossible now to conceive of, and yet before the Revolution he had been an honest, sober, decent, and even good man, a respectable mechanic in good circumstances, remarkable for his industry and orderly life, and his was the case of a large number, I may say of the greatest number. This shows how much those wicked and impious wretches were to be pitied

---

Death of the Rev. Mr. Gautier, of Brutz, and of the good Farmer who endeavoured to protect him.

The Rev. Mr. Gautier was, at the time of the Revolution, Vicar of the Parish of Brutz, about two leagues and a half from Rennes. Brutz was the first place in which I exercised the Holy Ministry, having been sent thither from the Seminary during the Easter Vacations in 1809 to assist the Parish Priest. This was sixteen years after the event which I am about to relate, and the memory of their good Vicar was still warm in the hearts of the Parishioners, and I well remember the sort of half-suppressed murmur in which they expressed their indignation against those who destroyed him, as if afraid to violate the injunction of forgiveness which their dying Pastor had imposed upon them.

He was betrayed in his hiding place during the terrors of 1793–94. The zealous and faithful friend who had concealed him attempted to resist his pursuers, and received a thrust of a sabre which caused all his bowels to fall out, and when conveyed away in company with Mr. Gautier he was unable to walk, and the Soldiers, having dragged him along for some distance in this state, were obliged to procure a cart in which they placed them. The Priest supported his poor friend across his knees, and in this manner heard his confession and prepared him for death. In this way they proceeded through the village of St. James, which is situated between Brutz and Rennes, the Soldiers marching on each side of the cart. How often in retracing their steps years afterwards has that scene come up before my mind's eye. Whilst passing through St. James the poor wounded man drew near his end, and Mr. Gautier informed the Soldiers of the fact, and entreated them to stop that he might die more quietly. His words touched their hard hearts, and they stopped the cart. Then Mr. Gautier drew forth his Ritual and the Holy Oils which he had with him, and there in the cart in the middle of the road, surrounded by those who were carrying him to death, he administered to the poor dying friend who had lost his life in endeavouring to save

his the Sacrament of Extreme Unction. A moment after the poor man breathed his last, and then they again urged on the horse. After all, to the eye of Faith, that poor cart, thus carrying the living and the dead, was their triumphal car, the one already gone to receive his reward and the other soon to follow him. As I have said, in passing along the same road afterwards I have often endeavoured to enter into the feelings of that good Priest, as in this way he was dragged along through the streets of Rennes, by the towers of St. Peter's, so familiar to him, where a short time before he would have received so many marks of respect on every side, and now so different: stopping before the municipality, and the mob gathering around and gazing at the victims—the Priest seated in the cart, and his dead friend lying beside him, a ghastly corpse. "Is he dead?" they ask; and then they utter their horrid jokes and some cry out, "To the Guillotine!" After some delay the corpse was taken out of the cart and disposed of, and Mr. Gautier was carried to prison (Des Portes Saint Michel).

Some days elapsed before he received his sentence. The new law, to hasten the execution within twenty-four hours after the capture, had not yet been published. Many of his parishioners came to visit him, and I have heard that the constant lesson to all of them was, pardon after his death for those who had denounced him and made known his hiding place to the authorities. I remember perfectly well that the day after he was guillotined, and received his crown of glory, the good Sisters of Charity, who were still permitted to serve the prisons, so difficult was it to find any one to replace them, sent to my mother a copy of Mr. Gautier's last testament or address to his parishioners, written the evening before his death. I had it a long time in my possession, but some way or other it has been lost. I remember how we often shed tears over it as we read those words of charity and faith and zeal for the cause of religion, then assailed with such desperate fury. He himself so calm, so happy to leave a world deluged with crimes, but so anxious for those he left behind him. I remember the solicitude of the good pastor and tender father, so sensible of the increasing danger of the times for the faith and piety of his flock. He insisted most on this point, and made appropriate exhortations to each class of his people—the aged, the married, the youths, the children, and at the conclusion several lines were taken up with the most fervent entreaties and solemn charges to forgiveness, urging on them the precept of our divine Lord, his own free and full pardon being expressed in the most affecting manner. Unfortunate denunciators! how must they have felt when these exhortations of their betrayed and murdered pastor came to their knowledge; for they must have heard of them, perhaps read them, for many copies were made and passed from hand to hand. And those of them also who survived those days of delirium, and who saw that religion which they hoped to root out rising in new majesty amidst the ruins of her desolate sanctuaries, and the bleaching bones of her holy martyrs—so much folly and barbarity, all useless, and they, as was often the case, obliged to seek an escape from the pangs of remorse at the feet of the successors of their victims. I remember a very striking case of this in the very Parish of Brutz of which Mr. Gautier [25] was the Vicar. The school-

[25] Father Carron, vol. iv. p. 44, mentions that M. Gautier was a native of the village of Calais, in the Parish of Forrè, and was born the 24th of March, 1764. After his ordination he was appointed Vicar of Brutz, and did not leave his Parish during the revolution, but remained in concealment, spending his nights in visiting his parishioners and administering to their wants. He was arrested in the park of the Château of Cicé. The young man who so generously sacrificed his life in endeavouring to protect M. Gautier was named Robloit.

Father Carron also gives a copy of M. Gautier's will, as follows :

In the name of the Father, and of the Son, and of the Holy Ghost.

I, Julien Paul René Gautier, during the last seven days confined in the prison near the Portes Saint Michel, at Rennes, and convinced that the end of my life is approaching, think it proper to leave in writing a few works expressive of my last wishes.

I request those who have anything belonging to me in their possession to send half of it to my dear mother as soon as they conveniently can, and to give the other half in charity to the poor, and to those who will pray to God for me, and for my relatives living and dead. But let no one who has in his possession anything belonging to me trouble himself about the matter. I do not intend to impose any burthen on their consciences; they will do the best they can, and that is enough. Iu distributing anything

master and head chorister was one of the few in that excellent Parish who had drunk of the cup of revolutionary madness. When I went there to

belonging to me, in charity, it is my wish that they would give the preference to those who belong to the Parish in which I had care of souls. It is of them I have received, and to them I ought to give.

I have in my heart at this moment all my dear Parishioners. I pray to the God of mercies to keep them in His grace. I do not wish that they would weep for me, but that they should weep for their own sins, and remember me in their prayers. Foı their consolation, let them remember that the life of man is but a smoke, which passes away in a moment, and which every one must leave sooner or later, and that blessed are those who have the happiness to shed their blood for Him who died for us all. Oh ! how great a grace, that a sinner like me should merit to suffer for the name of Jesus Christ. Oh ! my God, my beloved Saviour, your mercies to me are beyond measure. Why have I not served you more faithfully ?

I beg of you now to call to mind what I have so often spoken to you. Bear with patience and resignation the misfortunes which God has permitted to come upon you. Let there be no murmuring, no blasphemy, no rebellion against God, who has sent these calamities as a punishment for our sins. Weep bitterly on account of the deluge of crimes which surround you. Every one should hope that they may soon come to an end. Especially let no one allow any thoughts of revenge to enter into his heart. Revenge is unworthy of a Christian, who should not only forgive but pray for his enemies. Besides, they are in reality our best friends, they give us so many opportunities of manifesting our faith and confessing Jesus Christ. Happy are those who confess Him before men, He will confess them before His Father in Heaven ; and woe to those who deny Him before men, He will deny them before His heavenly Father. Let the young men keep quiet and attend to their work—idleness is the mother of all vices. Let them mix themselves up in public matters as little as possible. Be careful to sanctify the Sundays and Festivals. Avoid places of amusement, so dangerous at all times for the soul. Do not keep drinking shops ; it is very difficult for any one who follows that business to save his soul. In a word, do sincere penance for your past sins, and make good, strong resolutions for the future, so as not to fall again. God's grace will never be wanting to enable you to keep them, if you are faithful to it. Be careful to give good example one to another ; say your prayers with fervour and attention, add to them always acts of faith, and hope, and charity, and contrition. Live as Christians and you will die as Christians. It

assist M. Massiot, in 1809, I noticed his still clear and pleasing voice as he sang in the choir, and afterwards M. Massiot said to me, "Did you notice that old man who led the choir? He was one of the 'Bonnets Rouge' here, an infuriated Jacobin, and now, thanks be to the mercy of God, one of my best parishioners—so penitent a sinner, so humble and distressed at the remembrance of those days, although I never allude to it, and all instinctively avoid saying anything in his presence which may wound his feelings."

is a dreadful delusion to put off one's conversion to the hour of death. May God's holy name be praised, and may my sins be washed away in my blood!

I pray for those who are about to put me to death. I pardon, from the bottom of my heart, those who caused me to be arrested. I know them, but I will not name them. If hereafter you find out who they were, remember that it is my injunction that you do them no harm. I sincerely thank those who have done favours to me—may the good God reward them!

In conclusion, I recommend to God all my parishioners, who are so dear to me. I recommend to them my beloved mother. Let her remember that she brought me up for God, not for herself. Also, my brother, my sister, my nephews and nieces. I exhort them to live together in the closest friendship, and not to allow the love of earthly things to cause them to forget eternal things.

I had forgotten to recommend to your prayers him who lost his life in endeavouring to save mine—may his soul rest in peace!

Be strong in the Faith. I die innocent, but I die in the Holy Catholic Apostolic and Roman Religion, of which I have been an unworthy minister. I have a thousand things to say to you, but have no more time.

JULIEN GAUTIER,
Curé of Brutz,
14th July, 1794.

Mr. Massiot had himself been a confessor of the Faith, and an exile in those days, as I have noticed in the account of Mr. Touchet, whose Vicaire he was at St. Hélier.

Banishment of Mr. Delaitre.

One day a young man of the most pleasing and prepossessing countenance, full of candour and modesty, was recommended to my Mother by a friend as a Priest from the Department of Calvados (Caen), who, having been too closely hunted in his own country, had sought for rest and better security in our city. I of course became acquainted with him, and soon very intimate. Good Mr. Delaitre, how pleasing the hours and days we spent together! We studied together and then stole out into the country and roamed about, his tender piety making use of everything to turn towards God. I see his countenance now, as, full of enthusiasm and divine charity, he expressed to me his love for Religion and his willingness to suffer for it, although the attachment and anxiety of his friends made him take precautions. The persecution being still severe in the city, he left it and went to my Sister's, at La Chapelle Bouéxie. After a while, when the Law of Death for the Priests was changed into that of Banishment to the pestilential coast of Cayenne, he returned to Rennes and lived with Mr. Petysain, a pious merchant, passing as his Clerk. One day, however, as he was crossing the public square, a Spy from his own department recognized him and bade him follow him to the Municipality; from the Municipality he went to prison, and from the prison, where I often visited him and passed many pleasant moments, he was soon after sent to his doom on the pestilential lands of Cayenne. The morning of their departure I was awakened about 4 o'clock by a rap at the door. A poor countrywoman ran from the market, which was near the prison, to my Mother. "Oh! Madame Bruté, those good Priests are starting from St. Michael's (the name of the prison); the order has been given suddenly last night; they are all in the cart already." I ran there as quickly as I could; they were just leaving. I approached as near as I could; they were in an open wagon, seated on their trunks, surrounded by mounted Gendarmes; my dear Mr. Delaitre, with his serene and impressive countenance as usual. When he saw me he waved his hand toward me, raising up his eyes to heaven and his other hand, saying merely, "Deo Gratias, Deo Gratias," "Thanks be to God," and the cart moved on.

After a few months we heard that his health had yielded to the effects of the climate, and that he had left the land of his double exile for that better country where "the wicked cease from troubling and the weary are at rest."

Mr. Martien, or Martineau, a Brother of the Christian School of Mr. La Salle.

As I have mentioned, I usually went to the "Criminal Court," where the Priests were generally tried, but on one occasion I went to the "Military Tribunal," and was at the trial and condemnation of a Christian Brother. I have not a very distinct remembrance of the circumstances, though I can still see the tall, spare form of Mr. Martien, and hear his voice as he pleaded in vain before his persecutors. The trial took place in the evening, and the President of the Court was a kind of philosopher, who made a great affectation of wisdom, and often spoke at the club (Société Populaire). Several persons were arraigned at the same time, for some pretended conspiracy I think. Mr. Martien pleaded in his defence that he was not a Priest or an Ecclesiastic, in any sense of the word; that, although associated with others in a Religious Society, he was but a school-master and nothing more—a School-master devoted to the education of poor children, which, if they were sincere in their professions of attachment to the poor and the principles of fraternity, ought to be a claim on their gratitude. All this was very true; but this was a sort of fraternity and devotion to the poor they had no sympathy with, and notwithstanding the validity of his plea he was immediately condemned to death. He was, I think, from St. Malo, and had spent fourteen years in his humble but holy vocation as a teacher of the children of the poor.[26]

Father Kergaté.

The Rev. Father Kergaté, of the Society of Jesus, lived at Rennes during the persecutions of 1793. I remember his mild virtues; his emaciated countenance, which told of self-denial and mortification, but with such gentleness and politeness of manner as indicated the spirit of true holiness. The alarms and horrors of the times seemed not to affect his peace, though, being a Priest, he was necessarily a devoted victim. He could not bear the passionate

[26] The Christian Brothers, or Frères des Ecoles Chretiennes, were founded by the Venerable John Baptiste de la Salle, in 1679, for the education of poor children. They were reëstablished after the Revolution, and have charge at present of most of the Primary Schools in France. The Abbé John de la Mennais, brother of the celebrated Felicité de la Mennais, has also founded a somewhat similar Institute for the poorer villages, which need only a single Teacher, as the Christian Schools always send two together.

expressions which, in the secrecy of almost every family, were uttered against the authors of so many dreadful crimes and cruelties. "Speak not so," he would say to his friends, when they gave vent to their indignation and reproaches in his presence. "Why so much anger? What harm can they do us after all? The extreme effect of their rage will only be to send us the sooner to our happiness, and in the meanwhile they afford us continual occasions of acquiring merit, if we will only be careful to cherish in our souls the spirit of patience and sincere forgiveness. Do we not remember, and shall we not imitate our blessed Lord, who was *silent* in the hands of his tormentors? Nay, good souls! are not these unfortunate men, against whom you manifest so much severity, objects of solicitude and pity, rather than their victims? Think of the condition of *their souls*, in what horrid misery and danger they are, and your anger will soon change into compassion and tears of true charity. When you meet a poor creature all covered with abominable ulcers, is it anger you feel towards him? Would you take up a rod and strike the poor miserable object? Where is our faith, when we forget the condition of the soul, the only just measure of our feelings, if we are good Christians? God forbid that we should forget the excellency of the graces offered to us through them, and our only sorrow should be that these unhappy benefactors so far expose their own souls when they do but hasten and secure the bliss of ours. Pity! the most tender pity for them is our duty; all the rest is wrong, and faults of nature." Thus, or rather to this purpose, did that good and charitable Priest often speak. He died not long after Robespierre, when the persecution was greatly mitigated, yet still fierce enough against the Clergy, especially if caught in the exercise of their holy functions. To the last there were plenty of opportunities afforded them to practice good Father Kergaté's advice, and it required much grace, and a strong sense of religion and charity, not to give way to imprecations against such miscreants, committing all their atrocities also in the name of liberty and public virtue.

And yet Father Kergaté was right; and if we be good Christians, we will forgive and pray for our persecutors. The prayer of St. Stephen, the old fathers say, converted Saul. "*Si martyr Stephanus non orasset, Ecclesia Paulum hodie non haberet.*"

Two Brothers Condemned to Die together.

I remember being present one day when two brothers were condemned to death as enemies of the Republic. It was in 1793, during the height of the terror. They were peasants,[27] simple men of the

[27] It is often supposed that only the higher classes—the nobles and

field, the one a husband and father, the other younger and unmarried. The scene was very affecting, especially when they returned to the Prison after hearing the sentence which sent them to die to-

clergy—suffered in the revolutionary fury. "The republican Prudhomme, whose prepossessions led him to anything rather than an exaggeration of the horrors of the popular party, has given the following appalling account of the victims of the Revolution :

Noblemen,	1,278	
Noble women,	750	
Wives of labourers and artisans,	1,467	
Religieuses,	356	
Priests,	1,135	
Common persons, not nobles,	13,623—	
Guillotined by sentence of Revol. Tribunal,		18,603
Women died of premature child-birth,		3,400
In child-birth from grief,		348
Women killed in La Vendée,		15,000
Children killed in La Vendée,		22,000
Men slain in La Vendée,		900,000
Victims under Carrier at Nantes,		32,000
Of whom were :		
Children shot,	500	
Children drowned,	1,500	
Women shot,	264	
Women drowned,	500	
Priests shot,	300	
Priests drowned,	460	
Nobles drowned,	1,400	
Artisans drowned,	5,300	
Victims at Lyons,		31,000
Total,		1,022,351

"In this enumeration are not comprehended the massacres at Versailles, at the Abbey, the Carmes, or other prisons, on the 2d of September, the victims of the Glacière of Avignon, those shot at Toulon, Marseilles, or persons slain in the little town of Bedoin, of which the whole population perished.

"It is noticeable in this dismal catalogue, how large a proportion of

gether the next morning. They were in the prime of life, in the consciousness of honesty and innocence—the poor husband and father, in particular, wept bitterly. "Ah! my brother," said the younger one to him, "do not thus give way to grief; how happy rather are we, so soon to go to heaven!" "To be sure, my brother; but my poor wife and my children, what will become of them?" And he wept the more, though after with true resignation in his heart. "Weep not," insisted the younger; "do you think God will abandon them? and since we shall see Him so soon, will we not pray much for them there?" And so they went to death—and to heaven.

Mr. Boisleve.

Mr. Boisleve was a lawyer, and was regarded in the Parliament and courts of Rennes as the most eminent Jurist and the most clearheaded and able Counsellor at the Bar; not particularly distinguished

the victims of thé Revolution were persons in the middling and lower ranks of life. The priests and nobles guillotined are only 2,413, while the persons of plebeian origin exceed 13,000. The nobles and priests put to death at Nantes were only 2,160, while the infants drowned and shot are 2,000, the women 764, and the artisans 5,300. So rapidly in revolutionary convulsions does the career of cruelty reach the lower orders, and so widely is the carnage dealt out to them, compared with that which they have sought to inflict on their superiors."—*Alison's Hist., vol. i. p.* 310, *Am. ed.; Prudhomme Vic. de la Révol.: Chateaubriand Etud. Hist.*

as an orator, but the very light of his profession in matters of counsel. He was at the same time a living saint, a model of innocence and simplicity and antique manners—modest and affable in his deportment, disinterested and charitable in the exercise of his profession, and well known to all for his sincere piety and attachment to his Religion. Every morning he was present at the early mass,[28] celebrated

[28] The following remarks, headed "EARLY MASS," were among Bishop Bruté's papers:

In our France, when I was a child, there were so many churches and so many priests, that the holy sacrifice of the Mass was, as it were, at the door of every one. Almost all the people used to be present at Mass every morning, before the Revolution. It was so ages back, and it would be so still, O merciful Lord! if thy people had better known and made a better use of thy infinite love. But thou hast again shown mercy to them, and, notwithstanding all their ingratitude and wickedness, hast restored to them in a great measure thy former blessings. Early Mass is the joy of every faithful family; some of its members can generally be present at the morning sacrifice; great numbers do attend it again, early, all over our favored France. Oh! how many untold blessings are brought down from heaven by that "pure oblation" thus offered up all over the land, a holocaust of propitiation, impetration, and thanksgiving. When I was a child, many thousands must have heard Mass every morning in our city of Rennes—in some families all the members. There were nine persons, including the servants, in our household, and habitually they had all heard Mass before 8 o'clock, when we assembled for breakfast. My good mother was an early riser, and, having awakened the rest of the family, she was accustomed to go to the first Mass, or at any rate to the second, for the first Mass was as early as 4 o'clock in summer. There was always a Mass at that hour at the church of the Bonne Nouvelle of the Dominicans, called the Mass of the Travellers, at which those who were about starting on a journey, and those also who were going into the country on pleasure parties, were accustomed to be present. My mother often went to this Mass, and I remember hearing her say: "It is astonishing, my child, how many there were at the 'Messe des Voyageurs,' this morning." Before she left the house, she used to charge her maid to see that we all got up and were ready in time; and I now call to mind her pleasant, cheer-

before 5 o'clock in the Convent of the Dominicans, kneeling behind a pillar, absorbed in recollection, so as to touch every heart that noticed him. My impression is that every morning he went to communion (though of this I will not be certain, though my mother so often spoke to me of that worthy man), and then returning behind his pillar, and spending a short time in prayer, he would go home and give himself up to the conscientious discharge of the drudgery which his great reputation and extensive practice imposed on him. He made a rule never to take fees in the cases of widows and minors, and adhered to it even in those cases where the circumstances by no means required it.

Nothing can give a more striking evidence of the influence which his character had acquired upon the minds of all, than the fact that in the midst of the wildest fury of the revolution it prevailed over the fanaticism of the most infuriated Jacobins, and surrounded him by their involuntary respect. I remember a striking example of this which occurred one day. Mr. Boisleve was accustomed to take a walk by himself every day in the public promenade. One day as he was proceeding to the place he approached the corner of a street where a num-

ful look when she used to return towards 5 o'clock, and hurry us off to get our share in those precious early graces. She, with her day of labour and often of great anxiety before her, all brightened and cheered by the consolations of that first action of the day, the assisting at the adorable sacrifice.

ber of the most furious Jacobins were congregated together, engaged in a loud discussion. He saw them, and though, according to his custom, he made no effort to avoid them, yet he intended to go around them, when all at once, as he approached them, they opened the way for him right and left, and, taking off their hats and caps, they permitted him to pass through their ranks in silence, bowing slightly to him; he himself silent and almost frightened at these signs of respect, if anything could easily have moved his quiet and superior soul. The moment he had passed, they themselves were surprised at what they had done towards one whom, as they said, was "none of ours." It was, in truth, the sudden, involuntary acknowledgment of superior worth—the influence of a long and justly enjoyed reputation overpowering for a moment conscious vileness and wickedness. Mr. Boisleve was attacked by his last sickness in the height of the revolution, a short time after the decree had been issued of death to any Priest within twenty-four hours after being arrested. A friend, however, offered to procure him the assistance of a priest, in order that he might receive the last consoling and strengthening Sacrament of the Church. "No, my friend," answered Mr. Boisleve, "I have been a long time preparing for this moment; I will trust myself to God, and will not expose any of his ministers to lose their lives on my account, when their services are so much needed for others who have neglected perhaps to prepare for death." It was an heroic act of self-sacrifice in one of such ardent faith, who had such love and veneration above all for the Blessed Sacrament, thus to resign it at that moment; and so he died, as he had lived, the model of a fervent Christian. My mother knew him very intimately and revered him as a saint. He had been of great service to her, after my father's death. It is the more pleasing to recall his virtues, because so many who belonged to his profession acted differently in those days of madness.[29]

The Countesses de Renac and the Rev. Mr. Marechal.

Two sisters, the Countesses de Renac, unmarried ladies, between thirty and forty years of age, lived together in a handsome little hotel, facing the public promenade, called La Motte à Madame, in the city of Rennes. My mother was accustomed to take her morning walk there, and a few days before the events which I am about to relate one of the ladies beckoned to her to come near the house, and

[29] The bitterest and most blood-thirsty actors in the French Revolution had been lawyers—Robespierre, Danton, Carrier, Couthon, &c. It should be remembered, however, for the honour of human nature, that Malesherbes, Trouchet, and Décaze belonged to the same profession.

said to her: "Madame Bruté, would you like to assist at Mass to-day?" To be present at the holy Sacrifice was at that time an inestimable privilege, so long and generally had Catholics been deprived of it by the terrible persecution of those days, which had then become more severe on account of the decree lately put forth, and to which I have alluded in the previous sketch, imposing the "penalty of death upon those who lodged a Priest, and the Priest himself, within twenty-four hours after their arrest."

My mother, on account of these circumstances, declined to be present, and earnestly entreated them to be more cautious at such a fatal period, when they ought to be too happy if they could save the life of the Priest, and their own.

The Priest whom they had concealed in their hotel was the Rev. Mr. Marechal, a young, fervent, and well-informed man, about 35 years of age.

A few days after that but too much needed caution, for these good and zealous ladies, as well as the Priest himself, were too imprudent, their house was denounced to the authorities as certainly harbouring some of the devoted victims.

Valeray, one of the most active and blood-thirsty agents of the Revolutionary Committees, and who alone had made almost half of all the arrests which had taken place, was appointed to make the search. He had received information that the Priest there concealed was M. Marechal, who had been his school-mate and particular friend; the information was, in fact, so precise as to leave no doubt that he was in the Hotel. Valeray consequently went thither with some of his most active and trusty men, and made a most careful examination of the whole house, and yet after spending hours at the work, hunting over and over every corner from the cellar to the garret, nothing was found. The ladies were present, composed and on their guard against every cunning request or question.

At length Valeray, finding that he was likely to be defeated in his purpose, took the ladies aside, and said to them with consummate hypocrisy: "You see, Ladies, the ardour of my men; the denunciation is so positive that we have no doubt that Mr. Marechal is here. He will assuredly be discovered; I am most willing and anxious that he may escape, but without exposing myself; I am obliged to fulfil my commission and urge my men to a more exact and diligent search; there is but one chance for him, Ladies, and that is for you to tell me where the poor fellow is concealed—my old friend, my old schoolmate—so hard for me this duty! If you will tell me where it is, I will keep my men away from that particular spot."

The two ladies looked at one another; the moment of hesitation was remarked by Valeray. He insisted now more earnestly, with the most fervent protestations of his now settled purpose to save Mr.

Marechal, if they would but trust him so far, for his unfortunate friend, whose discovery would also be the doom of two ladies so much respected in the city, so much to be pitied. One of the ladies looked anxiously at the other, and by the expression of her countenance seemed to ask the other if they ought not to seize upon this chance of better security. The other, less trusting, answered by a forbidding and warning look; but the more confiding heart of her sister could not resist the eager entreaties of the man, and she pointed out to him the place of Mr. Marechal's concealment, which was no doubt behind some of those double walls or ceilings the contrivance of which was carried to a great perfection in those times. The persecutors were, however, seldom foiled; they had so many ways of finding out these hiding places[30] by measuring and sounding with long iron rods and pikes every suspicious corner. No sooner had the good lady given the desired hint, than Valeray called out with joy to his men to come and pull down the boards which concealed his victim; and as soon as he perceived the friend whom he had so wretchedly betrayed, he said to him: "I am sorry, my dear Marechal, that this office has fallen to me, but the will of the nation

[30] It is well known with how much ingenuity the Priests' hiding places were contrived in the houses of the Catholic nobility and gentry in England during the time of persecution. Almost all the old Catholic manor-houses boast of some such "Prophet's chamber in the wall."

must be carried out. We will soon see the last of your caste; come and follow me."

They were all, of course, immediately hurried to the Tribunal; the two noble ladies more afflicted at the fate of their excellent friend, and the unfortunate manner in which his capture had been brought about by their fatal confidence in the promise of that wicked man, than afraid to suffer, and receive the crown of Faith, of Charity, which became for so many in those times an object of envy and exalted desires.

What I have related so far is founded upon the information given to me at the time. As to what follows I was an ocular and hearing witness. As soon as I heard of their having been carried before the Tribunal, I followed them there and took my place close by the victims. The Priest was on one side, and was first called upon to answer; the ladies were seated on the opposite side. "Your name?" asked the President. "Write," said he, actually dictating to the clerk of the Tribunal, "that my name is Marechal." The clerk having written this down, the second question was put as usual, "Your profession?" and Mr. Marechal again dictated as if with the intention of preserving his replies from misrepresentation: "Write a Roman Catholic Apostolic Priest." The clerk turned with impatience to the President, and asked if he was obliged to write down this answer, which the citizen had dictated to him with so much coolness and formality. The President answered, "No matter, write it down as he spoke it." Two or three questions were then addressed to Mr. Marechal, which I have forgotten. I remember, however, that he stated with great calmness and force the principles which had caused him to refuse compliance with the requisitions of the law in regard to oaths, &c.; and that he manifested an uncommon degree of self-possession, moderation, and politeness during his short interrogatory.

The ladies were then called upon to answer in their turn. Unfortunately, I cannot now recall to mind the questions that were put to them, nor their answers; though when I went home from these strange scenes I could, as I have said, relate every word and circumstance. But although I cannot now recall what was said to them, probably only the ordinary questions, yet I can still see those two respectable ladies, wearing black caps and mantles, according to the fashion of the city—both tall, slender, pale, with mild and interesting countenances. The whole matter was, as usual, hurried over in the most expeditious manner; the law being clear and express, and allowing of no qualifications. The sentence of death was passed upon Mr. Marechal and the two ladies by the President of the Tribunal, Bouassier.[31] That unhappy man seemed

31 It would be very interesting to consult the Archives of the Tribunals

to be affected on this occasion. He knew the ladies well, and was conscious of all the injustice and horror of the deed he was committing; his countenance and voice became altered in the most frightful manner. I can distinctly see him now, as he appeared at that moment, and can hear his harsh, sad, angry voice. I remember that I pitied him more than I did his victims.

While the sentence was being pronounced, one of the sisters could not hear the awful word *death.* She fainted, and, falling from her seat, lay senseless upon the floor. Oh! what a sight, what a moment! All seemed affected. She was soon raised up, assisted, if I remember well, by Mr. Marechal and her sister, who united in this office with the Gendarmes. What occurred after this moment, until they left the court, is confused in my mind, and I do not wish to record anything except what I distinctly remember. They were soon led from the Tribunal to the Guillotine, and there I could never prevail upon myself to be present. I always hastened from the Tribunal to relate all that had occurred to the family and to other friends, trembling almost, whilst we mingled our tears together, lest some one should enter, or some traitor should

of those times, if they have been preserved—both the minutes of the examinations in manuscript and the printed judiciary sentences, which were posted on the walls throughout the city at each execution.—*MS. Note by Bp. Bruté.*

be at hand to denounce us. To manifest any pity towards the enemies of the Republic, or the Priests, or their fanatical devotees, as they were called, who endeavoured to protect them, was a sufficient cause for being denounced as "suspect," and there were no less than ten different constituted authorities who had power to commit persons thus suspected to prison, and many hundred persons were at that time crowded into these "prisons des suspects"—the men in the ancient Convent of the Trinity, and the women in an establishment called "The Good Shepherd," which had previously been a house of refuge for penitent females. I was informed that when the Countesses of Renac went up to the Scaffold they were supported and encouraged to the last by Mr. Marechal, who as being a Priest, the "most guilty," had to suffer death last. The one who fainted at the Tribunal fainted again on the Scaffold, and was guillotined in that condition, senseless and unconscious.

The President of the Tribunal, Bouassier, received such a shock in this particular case that his health was ever afterwards vitally affected; his pale, bilious, and emaciated face, his hollow voice and frequent sighs, all marked the anguish of his poor soul. When Buonaparte came into power, he was continued in his place as Judge and President of the Court, I think; but, according to the stories which circulated at the time, life was a great burthen to him, and his existence very miserable. One day, several years after the events above related had taken place, he was taking a solitary walk on that very spot, La Motte à Madame, opposite to which stood the Hotel de Renac, when suddenly he heard his name called, Bouassier; he turned round, but seeing nobody, he continued his walk to the other end of the alley, where a second time he heard Bouassier. This alarmed him, but he continued his walk, when a third time he heard his name plainly called, Bouassier, and then, in the utmost agitation and alarm, he turned to some young men whom he saw approaching, and who perhaps he thought were playing some trick upon him. "What is the matter, gentlemen; why am I called?" "The matter, Sir!" they answered; "don't you perceive it is the voice of the ladies at that hotel?" pointing to the Hotel de Renac. Bouassier returned home in the greatest distress of mind, and, I think, fell sick immediately; certain it is that he died a short time after this event, and there is a circumstance still more remarkable connected with his death which I must not pass over. During his last illness he was attended by Dr. Dulattay, his old friend, an excellent physician and a very religious man. The evening before he died the Doctor, seeing how low he was, said to him: "My dear Bouassier, you are very ill indeed, and have but a short time to live; would you not like to see one of our old friends—for instance, Father Gaffard?" Father Gaffard was a Carmelite, and had been the schoolmate of both; he was a very learned man, and noted for his moderation and amiability in the discharge of his duties. "Oh, yes," said the unfortunate dying man, "it would afford me great happiness." The doctor immediately went in search of Father Gaffard, and at 11 o'c. at night, if I remember rightly, the good Father hastened with anxious joy to save, if possible, their former persecutor. What happiness for any Priest, still more for one who had been his friend in better days; but, oh! what a terrible judgment of God, when he, who had so cruelly put them to death, wanted a Priest, he was not permitted to have that blessing! His own son, who had been brought up by him in the school of Voltaire and Rousseau, and who had been himself conspicuous amongst the most infuriated Jacobins during the horrid times of Robespierre, stood in the way. He received Father Gaffard with the most angry countenance, told him that his father was a better man than himself (the Priest) and needed none of his assistance to die properly. Father Gaffard pleaded in vain, and was not permitted to enter. Bouassier died that night. May his desire have been received, and his victims have enjoyed the happiness of meeting him in Heaven, for whom they had so often and so fervently poured forth their prayers with their very blood!

The above circumstances were related to me, at the time, by those who had an opportunity of knowing them, and I have no doubt of their truth.[32]

Incidents connected with the War in La Vendée.

There is not in history a greater contrast than that presented between the Vendéans and their oppressors. The one side is an exhibition of everything that dignifies human nature, the other of everything that degrades and debases it. A virtuous and brave peasantry fighting for their altars and firesides without arms, and unacquainted with military discipline, and yet overthrowing and driving back large and powerful armies, returning the cruelties inflicted upon them by kindness when victorious. Such is the picture presented by the peasants of La Vendée. On the other hand, the cruelties practised upon them is one of the darkest shades in the dark picture of the French Revolution. Cathelineau the virtuous peasant, who was the first General of the Vendéans, and the infamous

Tresvaux, vol. ii. p. 108, relates the same circumstances in regard to the death of Bouassier, and says that they were told to him by very respectable persons, as having been well known to every one at the time.

Carrier, the author of the noyades at Nantes, may stand as types of the two parties.[33]

In 1793 the National Convention, maddened apparently by the successful resistance of the peasants of La Vendée, issued a decree of desolation against the province—the villages to be burned, the men put to death wherever found, and the women and children to be removed into the interior of France.

Vast numbers passed through our city of Rennes on the way to their place of banishment, and often

[33] There are no brighter pages in the annals of heroism than those which record the struggles of the peasants of La Vendée, in defence of their homes and their religion, against the revolutionary armies. The insurrection commenced in Anjou, on the occasion of the conscription (300,000 men were demanded for the army). It originated with the peasants themselves. "The unhappy peasants," says Madame De la Rochejaquelin, "wounded in everything that was dear to them, subjected to a yoke which the happiness they had formerly enjoyed made them feel still heavier, revolted at last, and chose for their leaders men in whom they had placed their confidence and their affection. The Gentlemen and Parish Priests, proscribed and persecuted themselves, marched with them and supported their courage. The insurrection began, from the impulse of the moment, without plan, without concert, and almost without hopes," and yet it took the whole power of Republican France to put it down. Cathelineau, their first leader, was himself a peasant. Their piety and moderation equalled their courage. At one time the insurgent country was surrounded by 240,000 Republican troops. If the English had coöperated with them at this time as they ought to have done, all the long wars and waste of money which followed might have been avoided.

La Vendée, properly speaking, included a portion of Poitou, Anjou, and the county of Nantes, known before the Revolution as the "Le pays du Bocage." It was on the other side of the Loire from Brittany, with which many persons confound it. Those who rose up against the Revolution in Brittany were called *Chouans*. They manifested equal bravery, but were not so humane as the Vendéans. The cruelties of the Revolutionary leaders and soldiers excited them at length to a pretty severe application of the *lex talionis*.

being obliged to halt for a short time, they were billeted for lodgings amongst the various families of the city. On one occasion a poor woman, her two daughters and a servant maid, were sent to our house, and permitted to rest themselves for a few days before proceeding on their journey. Their destination, if I remember rightly, was Caen, in the ancient province of Normandy. Poor indeed they were; before leaving home they had seen the same house which had so long sheltered them, and in which they had enjoyed so many happy hours, burnt to the ground—the fields spoiled and devastated—the husband and father fled to the Vendéan army, and in all probability they were never to see him again, perhaps never hear of his fate. The good wife was perhaps forty years of age, or rather less—the picture of a fine healthy woman, now worn out by fatigue and anxiety, soon to be quite broken down by sorrow. The two daughters, 16 and 18, one taller than the mother, bearing in their countenances and all their conduct the evidences of the virtuous domestic training they had received—so modest and retiring, and yet so courageous, and so full of tender affection and respect for their mother. The one that pleased me most, however, was the strong, single-hearted servant maid, so humble, so faithful, and yet so little conscious of her worth. The friend now—once evidently the trusted and kindly treated servant at home, and now the best of friends. When the mistress knew of their doom, she sent her servant man, with a small sum of money, to go to Nantes by byways, to wait for their passage, when the "infernal column," as it was justly called, should come to execute the decree to destroy their property and drive them from home. When the party that came to their house had done their work, and carried them to Nantes, she sought for the trusted servant; but a few days and temptation had wrought a great change in him—he denied the deposit, and threatened if they said anything about the matter, to denounce them to the authorities. At that cruel moment the poor mistress turned to her maid and said, "Now, my child, you will have to leave us. I have no longer the means of recompensing you for your services. You are strong, and can easily obtain permission to remain in Nantes, and find some means of supporting yourself. As for my daughters and myself, misery is our doom; we must go on, and abandon ourselves into the hands of Providence." "Not so, good mistress," was the answer of the poor girl. "I will not leave you, and what I can earn shall be for us all"; and so it was. The tears start to my eyes now as I recall with what expressions of tenderness the afflicted mistress dwelt upon the devotion and fidelity and laborious services of the good handmaid, wherever they had been. I remember that even during the few days they stayed with us the faithful servant endeavoured to find some work in the city, in order to supply funds to assist the family in their further wanderings. My mother pitied and respected them, and did all that was in her power to protect and aid them. It was the more sad for them, for at the same time no less than fourteen soldiers were billeted upon us—a party of those very men who had just been committing such horrors in La Vendée, and amidst their riotings their chief occupation was to boast of what they had done, taking pleasure apparently in rehearsing their basest and most abominable deeds, so that these poor Vendéan exiles, notwithstanding all the care of my mother, were obliged, more or less, to listen to these heart-rending details, and to have their wounds opened afresh, for nothing made these monsters worse than the sight of their victims.[34]

Mr. Joyaux and the Prince of Rieux.

Mr. Joyaux was the Intendant, as it was called, oi the Château and domains of the Prince of Rieux,

[34] Madame De la Rochejaquelin, (Memoir, p. 408, et seq.,) dwells with grateful enthusiasm upon the generous hospitality with which the Breton peasants and others sheltered the refugees from La Vendée. "Although many of them," she says, "were put to death for having offered an asylum to the Vendéans, this did not diminish the devoted attachment which men, women, and even children, seemed to feel for us, nor cool their active humanity."

about 50 miles from Rennes. The last time I saw this excellent and most respectable man, the shadow of death was hovering over him, and it was reflected from every feature of his face. He was dying literally of sorrow—brought upon him by the events of those sad days, and which was so profound as to have triumphed over the best efforts of his virtuous and religious soul: the proscription of Religion—the slaughter of so many Priests—the destruction of so many noble and ancient families, who had been so much respected and loved in our Brittany. But the event which put the last bitter drop in his cup of affliction was the fatal end of the expedition of Quiberon. Amongst those who were put to death on that occasion, after having capitulated, was the young Prince de Rieux, the last of that ancient family, and one every way worthy to transmit their name with honour. What made it more sad, was that he would have escaped had it not been for an almost unavoidable mistake made by Mr. Joyaux himself, the most devoted adherent and friend of the young Prince, and who would gladly have laid down his own life for him. When the prisoners had capitulated they were led to Auray,[35] a few miles distant from the place of the action, where

Monseigneur de Hercé, the Bishop of Dol, the Count de Sombreuil, who commanded the troops, and a large number of noblemen and Priests, who belonged to the unfortunate expedition of Quiberon, were put to death, in violation of the capitulation, in a large field or meadow near the city of Auray. The place has since borne the name of the "Field of Marthey were confined under a strong guard. After a mock trial they were condemned to death as Emigrés, and taken out by detachments to be shot. Still, even in this short interval many escaped, some by accident, as it were, in the midst of the confusion, and some by bribing the soldiers. Mr. Joyaux was at Rieux, the manor of the young Prince, about twenty miles from Auray, when he received a letter, written by a common and zealous friend: "Come immediately and bring 3,000 francs, and you can save the Prince"; but on the back was written, by some strange fatality: "You will be too late; before you arrive the Prince will be shot." Overcome by his feelings, Mr. Joyaux dropped the letter, and thinking all was over, gave himself up to his sorrow, and it was not until two or three hours had been lost that, recovering from his despair, it occurred to him that he ought to have gone at any rate. He immediately set off with the money, and found, on arriving at Auray, that if he had arrived a few minutes sooner he would have been in time. The Prince had just been shot. The affectionate heart of the good old man was broken, and the faithful friend soon followed his beloved young Prince. "He was the last, Madame," I remember hearing him say to my mother; "he was the last, the hope of that ancient and noble race, and I was

tyrs." A chapel has been erected near the spot, and the remains of those who perished collected, as far as possible, and placed within it

the cause of his death by my fatal delay. Oh! that fatal postscript." No reasoning nor words of consolation could assuage the sorrow which preyed upon him. He lost his appetite, could eat nothing, and a few months after he died. One of Mr. Joyaux's sons afterwards lost his life in the royal cause.

Armand de Montluc.

I was at school in my youth with Armand de Montluc, the son of one of the most ancient and richest families of our nobility. He had a mild and amiable disposition, a very agreeable countenance, a pious heart, and was much beloved by all of us. Of his charity to the poor, the virtue of all his family, I recall many instances which came to my knowledge. How many others are unknown! When very young his father gave him a louis-d'or (a guinea) for pocket money. The day after the washer-woman, a poor widow with a family, found it in the foot of one of his stockings, put there designedly by our good Armand, who thought in his simplicity that she would keep it, and he have the merit of a good action without the praise. The poor woman understood the whole matter as soon as she found the money, and brought it to the Duchess with tears of pleasure and admiration running down her cheeks. Armand's gift was ratified by his parents, and from that time they provided for all the wants of his poor old protegée. Dear Armand! he died young, in exile, obliged like so many others to flee from France.

His father and mother also died in exile—the most charitable and beneficent persons in our city. Madame de Montluc (though I was very young then, yet I retain a most vivid recollection of her features and appearance, of small stature, a most placid, pleasing countenance and gentle manners) not only bestowed upon the poor, with the consent of her worthy husband, for they were of one heart in all these matters, a considerable portion of their income, but regularly visited them at their homes, and attended them in their sickness, rendering to them personally every office of charity with her own hands. She overcame every natural repugnance, and was deterred by no danger. At one time our city was visited by disease of a very contagious and disgusting character, but this good lady only manifested the greater zeal. She was everywhere, attending upon those who were attacked by it, until at length an attached servant who used to accompany her was so overpowered by repugnance and the fears of death that he actually refused to go with her any more, and she continued to go alone and perform the most menial and often disgusting offices.

The well-known Mademoiselle de Cicé was a

Sister of Madame de Montluc. She resided in Paris, and was a truly holy woman, so devoted to deeds of charity that she could not avoid being known and esteemed. This excellent woman was on a very remarkable occasion tried for her life, and came very near losing it, from the horror she had of committing a venial sin, by telling an officious lie, to save herself.[36] In vain did her counsel represent to her the legal course of things, and the danger to which the positive enactment of the law exposed her; the judges, whatever they might think or feel, being obliged to go the full length of their inflexible line. She could not be persuaded to deviate in the least, by a positive untruth, from the facts as they were known to her. Her beautiful candour was, after all, her protection. It excited the admiration of every one in the court, and

[36] I find the following circumstance related by Bp. Bruté, in one of his Letters to Bp. Kenrick; speaking of the officious lie, he says: "It may afford you pleasure to be made acquainted with the conduct of one of the most eminent magistrates of the Parliament of Paris, who suffered death rather than to tell an officious lie. Mr. Augran d'Alleray, the gentleman to whom I allude, and who was equally distinguished by his piety and eminent talents, had been accused and arrested on the charge of sending money to his son, who had emigrated, contrary to the law. To acknowledge that he had done so was certain death. The famous, or rather infamous, Fouquier-Tainville, the public prosecutor, notwithstanding his ferocity, wished to save Mr. d'Alleray's life, and tried to get him to deny it. But this excellent man could not bring himself to tell a lie even to save his life. 'Wast thou ignorant, citizen,' said the ferocious judge, 'of the law which forbade you to do it?' 'No,' answered he, 'I was not; but I knew of a law still more sacred—that of nature, which commands a father to succor his children.' This noble and touching answer was the cause of his death; he was guillotined in 1794, aged 79 years."

the effect was heightened by the charming simplicity and modesty of her whole demeanour in so critical a situation. Her account of the matter was received, though unsupported by any other evidence, and she was released, after having obtained the whole merit of such a beautiful sacrifice of pure love for God.[37]

[37] I find appended to the above relation the following memoranda, made by some one who has looked over these papers, but whose handwriting I am unacquainted with—probably a French Priest of the Diocese of Vincennes:

"The author of this sketch of Mademoiselle de Cicé's trial ought not to have omitted to mention that this trial was relative to an attempt to assassinate Buonaparte, called the Plot of the Infernal Machine (24th December, 1800). Mademoiselle de Cicé was accused of having procured a lodging for a man concerned in the plot, though she knew nothing of him, but had done it at the recommendation of a most respected clergyman. Summoned to declare the name of that clergyman who had recommended the man to her charity, she said that in telling his name she would infallibly deliver him to the same prosecutions and dangers to which she and the two ladies (Mesdames de Goyon, mother and daughter) were exposed, whom she had brought in that distress, but who knew nothing more than herself of the man, and that the gentleman who had recommended him to her charity was purely as innocent as themselves: wherefore she would not cause one more misfortune. No threats, no danger, no supplications were ever able to draw anything else from her, and she was acquitted from complicity, not only by the universal admiration created in the court, not only by the generosity of her silence and her meek deportment, but by the depositions of some two hundred poor, or sick, or anywise unfortunate persons of all the quarters of Paris, without distinction of opinions, who declared that they were indebted to her charity or assistance for relief in their respective circumstances.

"She was at that time the Mother Superior of the pious Association of the Ladies of the Sacred Heart of Mary, formed since the beginning of the revolution, with the view of supplying to the religious orders, which were destroyed, and presenting to pious women, the means of professing religious perfection, without being subject to the control of the civil authority, just as the Society of the Sacred Heart of Jesus opened to religious men the same opportunity.

Our Sundays in 1793.

In carrying my remembrances back to those sad days of which I am writing, I recognize that I never have thanked God as I ought to have done for those particular graces by which he preserved me in the midst of so great madness and impiety. Those who were at the head of the irreligious frenzy which then devastated our France pressed forward with all the confidence of success. Every device of cruelty and malice was put in operation to attain the end they had in view, viz.: to destroy the Catholic Religion, not only in France but throughout the world. So far, as I am witness, did their detestable hopes of the complete final triumph over the Christian Faith extend.

"Mademoiselle de Cicé died in 1818 or '19. The celebrated Monsig. Champion de Cicé, Archbishop of Bordeaux, and after the Concordat, of Aix, was her brother. Another of her brothers was Bishop of Auxerre. The pious Abbé Carron has written an abridgment of her life."

"My good friend, the author of the Sketches, who has joined examples of religious fortitude and constancy in some laymen, particularly in Mr. Boisleve, may have known also Mr. de la Chevallaray, at Rennes. Still young, but of age to bear arms, it was proved that he had corresponded with his brother, who was an *émigré*, and was accused of having sent money to him (a charity which was at that time punished by death). 'No,' said he, 'I have not sent money to him, because I had not the means.' He was summoned to enlist or to take up arms for the nation. He refused and was put in prison; the judge urged him to get a substitute, or pay the expense of one. 'I shall no more pay for doing evil,' said he, 'than I will do it myself.' Threatened with losing his liberty or his estate, he said, they could dispose of his body and his goods as they pleased, but he would save his soul.

"I saw this gentleman at Rennes in 1798; he was an example of piety, constancy, and calmness of mind in the midst of these horrid times."

And yet, at that very moment, how strong and imperishable was its hold upon thousands of hearts; how fervently did every true Christian family pledge its love and life to our blessed Lord; how constantly did Christian mothers require of their offspring that, no matter what happened, they would never forget their duty to God! With how much anxiety, and yet fidelity, did they endeavour, especially on Sundays, to supply the want of the publick exercises of Religion and sanctify the day in their family! How many touching remembrances come crowding into my mind, connected with those acts of fidelity to God in the midst of the dark days which brooded over us! Death, prison, exile, were the penalties. The decrees in which they were set forth were posted at every corner, and every day witnessed how severely and unmercifully they were enforced. Every city and town, and almost every village, had its "Committee of Publick Safety," as it was called, armed with the most arbitrary authority, in the name of *Liberty*, and exercising it with a vigilance and energy which rendered it at length almost impossible for any number of Catholics to meet together for Mass, or any other office of Religion. The Priests, as was to be expected, were the particular objects of their hatred, and the greatest caution and most secret hiding places could not save them from the grasp of a host of informers and blood-thirsty monsters, who almost any day had an execution to gratify their malice and encourage their pursuits. Even in those families who had a Priest concealed in their house, it was often thought best not to hazard any celebration of the Holy Sacrifice within doors; so great was the danger and so controlling the terror, that in many families all the members were not made acquainted with the presence of the good man, whom some of the most resolute members ventured to keep concealed in the face of death—death for the Priest, and death for those who thus harboured the victims and endeavoured to keep alive the last hopes of Religion; the last hopes, indeed, they seemed, so few in number and every day diminishing. No Bishops, no Seminaries, no means of supplying the gaps made. And then the malignity and power of those who were labouring to erect Philosophy, as they called it, on the ruins of Fanaticism, filling the eyes of our poor youth with their gigantic efforts and boundless confidence. Every avenue of good choked up or destroyed, and every evil influence permitted to have full sway. Their very songs, all the day long, in the shops and streets, filled with insult and derision of the Clergy and the ancient faith of the French nation, and often expressing their triumph at what they believed to be its utter destruction. Those days are now happily gone, but oh! how dreadful they were while they lasted.

On Sunday, my mother always summoned us, before breakfast, usually to the parlour, and there kneeling before a large ivory Crucifix (on black velvet), which she brought from her small oratory, she would begin the Prayers of Mass, with such a sad affecting voice, reading them out of her large favourite Prayer Book (Heures à la Chancellier); they were truly beautiful prayers. One is often in my mind—at the Preface—"Voic il'heureux moment où le Roi des Anges, et des hommes, va paraître—que mon cœur dégagé de la Terre, ne pense qu'à vous, O mon Dieu! le remplir de votre amour," etc. The King of men and angels was indeed present, invisibly, but not, alas! to be present in the divine Sacrament of love. No, alas! no Priest—no Altar, was there. Young as I was, I remember how sad, how desolate everything seemed without that living presence; but how strongly did even this desolation seem to bind my heart to our holy religion! And how holy and revered did my good mother become to me, as with her sad, grave voice, she fervently read the beautiful prayers and made the acts of Faith, Hope, and Charity, at a time when all those virtues acquired additional merit by the test they were put to!

More in regard to our Sundays in 1793.

"Come, it is seven o'clock"; and we all followed mother to the Drawing-room; sometimes to another room more retired. "Has Julian come?" she would ask. Julian was the gardener, and came on Sundays from our house in the suburbs. Julian and his wife would make their appearance, and the servants from the other parts of the house. Then we would all kneel, and sometimes mother would say a few words, before beginning, in regard to directing our attention, &c.; at other times she would say nothing; then a pause, save here and there a sigh—some with faces hid in their hands; and then she would commence, "In the name of the Father and of the Son and of the Holy Ghost." All of us making the sign of the Cross together, and then she would go on with the service. All stood at the Gospel; we stopped in silence at the time marked for the Consecration. My mother's voice is still sounding in my ears; her very accents are as present to me at this moment as if I was still listening to them, as with a tranquil and grave manner, and with a tone of unaffected but overawed piety, she went through the service. I remember that sometimes she would give a deep sigh—it could not have been otherwise, from a heart weighed down by so many present horrors, with such sad anticipations for the future—the *past* so dear to her, adding to the anguish of her nobly religious, motherly, and patriotic soul. At that age, although very strongly impressed, I could not of course feel all that my good mother felt. Oftentimes whilst kneeling there we could hear the sound of the drums from afar—and sometimes under our very windows, as the troops came to prepare for a review in the Square before our residence ; and not unfrequently we were disturbed by the noise and tumult attending upon the capture of a Priest, or other persons obnoxious to the authorities, and whom they were bringing to be tried and executed. One object of horror was always there, the Guillotine, which stood "en permanence," as they called it, on the Square near the Tribunal, and upon which every day some victim of revolution was sacrificed, not unfrequently persons well known to us, or related to us. Among such scenes, and under the influence of such events and associations, it was that we performed our religious duties, as well as we could.

After the Prayers of Mass mother would either read an Instruction for us or make me read one. I think I was generally the reader. Mostly they were from a work by Mgr. Fitz-James, Bishop of Soissons, entitled, "Instructions for all the Sundays and Festivals of the Year."

Sometimes I spent the Sunday at my Sister's, of whom I have already spoken, at La Chapelle Bouéxie. It was a vast Château, one of the most considerable in the Province, with a large estate, of which her husband was the Intendant. The property belonged to the Marquis de Poineaux. He was not an emigrant, but lived half in concealment, either at Paris or in other parts of France, where the family had possessions. My Sister assembled all the people in the great hall, and was, like my mother, at Rennes, the family Priest; no less strictly devout and careful; though I remember that her voice of call and command, to gather us all together, before beginning, was not so positive nor so much of the pontifical kind as my mother's. Her husband, although a very religious man, was never present, nor officiated. Though a man, and of a strong mind, he had so much sensibility that the scenes and associations always overcame him, and he could not trust himself. I remember in particular that one Sunday after the service was finished, as I went up-stairs, I met him coming from another apartment. "Gabriel," he said to me, "be not surprised at my absence; I cannot attend; my tears get the better of me." And then he began to repeat some verses from the Psalms which he had been reading, and went on to express his horror of the present impiety, his attachment to the Catholic faith, and his determination to do everything in his power to bring up his family in it.

Such were the Sundays of those times.

The Hospital of the Incurables.

Among the fruits of that old Catholic faith which our *philosophers* hoped to destroy I might mention the good Sisters of the Incurables. I know not what brings them into my mind at this moment, except the thought that the Catholic Church alone has ever produced such persons. All other devotion and heroism and self-sacrifice fades before theirs.

Our Hospital of the Incurables at Rennes was a miserable place. The site had been badly chosen, in a low, damp situation. The building itself was large and sufficiently commodious. You entered a large, oblong yard, before the building, after the French manner; at the gate was the "Tronc des pauvres malades": the gatekeeper, a fair sample of the inmates, a poor, battered old hulk, who had been nearly knocked to pieces in the voyage of life, and was now moored here for the rest of his term. As you crossed the yard you met many wandering about, all bearing evidences in their faces or limbs of the diseases which had brought them to this their last earthly home—for the certificate of admission required a positive declaration of real incurability. Within two large halls for the patients, about one hundred beds, I think, each with its four posts and green curtains. In the middle, facing the front, large folding doors opened into the Chapel, which extended back into the garden. When these doors were opened the Altar could be seen from a great number of the beds on the opposite side; and there on that altar was the only sight to console hopeless misery. One poor girl, about twenty years of age, I still remember—who was afflicted with the most extensive, horrid ulcer, monstrously swelled—the pains excruciating, so that no patience or resignation could prevent her crying and sobbing, even at the anticipation of having it dressed, how much more so whilst it was being dressed, as it had to be every day with the greatest care. The case was a peculiar one, and the physicians had devoted to her every attention and exerted all their skill for many months, at the other hospital, but in vain; and now she had been transferred to the Incurables as a hopeless case. Her bed, I remember, was happily opposite the opening of those sacred doors, so that from it she beheld the throne of mercy and of consolation. And oh! how much did those poor sufferers, nailed for the remainder of their lives to such heavy crosses, need such consolation; and then often, also, the Divine Victim came from the Altar to visit them in their bed of pain and to unite himself more intimately to them, and give them grace and strength to carry those crosses after him. Oh! how abundant are the alleviations provided for the poor and suffering in God's holy Church. And then those Sisters, those living angels who waited on them and rendered to them every office of love and kindness, with a mother's tenderness. As I recall them now, moving about so placidly, with such cheerful patience, my heart is moved, even at such a distance of time and place, to feelings of the most ardent respect and affection. With what pleasure did I visit you, blessed souls! when I returned to our France in 1815—you, my dear Sister Desprez—and you, good mother of your humble Sisters, Madame Meneast—God bless you and prosper you, to eternal crowns! The Sisters of the Incurables in our city of Rennes, as in many other similar establishments in various parts of France, belonged to no particular religious order or congregation. They were formed merely by a simple union of four or five or more pious souls, devoting themselves to this particular charity. It seems they are never at a loss for members to continue their holy work as they may be needed. I know not how long they have existed at Rennes in this manner, nor who is their Superior, nor what vows they take; but I know that they have always been there, in my day, at their painful but holy task, except for a short time when the friends of liberty, equality, and fraternity dispensed with their services. Their dress a plain grey; a coarse apron of white linen; their coiffe, or head-dress, called *Catiole*, the same with that of the common people.

Sister Desprez, of whom I have spoken above, belonged to a very respectable family in Rennes. She had inherited considerable property from an aunt, and was in the enjoyment of every comfort in this life, but our Lord called her with His gentle voice of special love to give up all and follow Him to His abode at the sad Hospital of the Incurables; the most trying and disagreeable of all our hospitals, situated moreover, as I have said, in a low, marshy place—they were always going to move it to a better situation, but somehow or other they never did. But when good Mademoiselle Desprez heard the *voice* this did not keep her back. She did not say, *if* they will remove the establishment to a more healthy place, or *if* I was stronger and had a better constitution (she was physically a poor, weak little body), or if, my Lord, you will be pleased to call me to some one of your other mansions. These thoughts and many others, very prudent and wise, such no doubt as the young man in the Gospel had who refused to sell all to follow our blessed Lord, may have come into her mind, but she did not listen to them. She did give up all and follow Him, and shut herself up for the rest of her life with the Incurables; and I remember that those who knew her intimately remarked how great graces God bestowed on her, as the immediate reward of her self-sacrifices and devotion. She had always been good and kind, but God now seemed to have lavished upon her all these blessed treasures of tenderness and cheerfulness which she would need for her poor incurables. It beamed from her eyes, was marked in her smile, and rendered her from the first moment a true *Religieuse* and perfect nurse. I do not exaggerate at all, for I witnessed it myself. Her plain and naturally unattractive face became radiant with a heavenly serenity and comeliness, her voice appeared as that of an angel, for kindness, and her manner so cheering and at the same time tranquillizing, nothing could be more pleasing. In fact, it was noticed that there was something peculiar, and more than usual even in religious women, in the admirable and not easily described dispositions of the Sisters of the Incurables. I often visited them with my mother. "Voyez, mon fils," she would say to me, "quelle serenité, quel air de contentement, ou voyez vous le pareil dans le monde, c'est etonnant"—and yet in reality not astonishing, when one reflects on the promise of our Lord to give an hundred-fold of consolation and peace to those who leave everything for His sake; but truly astonishing to those who are not in the line of those graces, and dwell only on the various disgusting and incurable diseases, and which it is their daily and nightly task to alleviate, not to cure, breathe that sickening atmosphere, which no attention can prevent or dispel.

These recollections of good Sister Desprez call to my mind Sister Magdalen of the Sisters of Charity, who for forty years had served the prisoners confined in the narrow and confined Prison of St. Michael's Gate at Rennes. She went to the prison in the morning and remained there until noon, and from one hour after dinner until night, shut up with her dear prisoners, as she used to call them, generally about 150 in number. She was very old and not very handsome when I knew her; but if handsome is who handsome does, then Sister Magdalen was beautiful. She was beautiful, at any rate, in the sight of the Angels. The kind words and kind works of forty years, bestowed often upon the ungrateful and repining, had given to her aged and wrinkled face an air of benignity and patience which no one could have passed by unnoticed. But the Revolution reached even Sister Magdalen in the prison. Her dear prisoners were let loose to become *citizens;* to enjoy the reign of equality and liberty—and the Priests and persons like Sister Magdalen were put in their place at St. Michael's Gate. It would have been no hardship, however, to Sister Magdalen to be shut up in prison, so they turned her out on the world, with which she had had nothing to do for half a century. I remember well when Sister Bonne, the Superior of the Sisters, or Sister Servant, as *they* call it, brought Sister Magdalen to my mother's house, the day they were turned out of their old home by the revolutionists. She came and stood before my mother in the parlor, looking at her and sighing a little, but saying nothing. She had not been accustomed to talk, except to her prisoners. In the evening she told my mother that it was the first day for forty years, except during the Retreats, that she had missed visiting the prison, and that she had never passed a day which seemed so long and tired her so much as that, her first day of idleness. Poor Sister Magdalen stayed with us a long while, and we would often have been tempted to laugh at her simplicity, and want of knowledge of the world, had it not been for the great respect which mother showed towards her.

Thirty Years, and more, Ago.

We lived then in the Parliament House of Brittany—a large and on the whole noble pile of buildings. It so happened that the Chapel of the Palace was situated immediately over our apartments. Forty or fifty granite steps led up to an immense Gallery fronting the public square. This gallery or hall was used for public meetings. At the end, over our apartments, as I have said, was the *Chapel.* Generally it was a solitude, for usually Mass was only celebrated in it once a year, at the opening of the Courts of Law after the vacations, when a Mass of the Holy Ghost was said to invoke a blessing on their labors; sometimes, though very seldom, for other purposes. One of my earliest and faintest recollections was assisting at Mass there, when my elder sister was married to Mr. Mazois. I was then only four or five years old. So near a Church, as it were, under the Altar and amidst the pillars which supported it, did I enter upon life; and nearer still, afterwards, did persecution bring the precious Altar of our Lord. Under that Chapel, and, more precisely still, in the room immediately beneath its sanctuary, did we erect our secret altar, during the dark days of the Revolution, where two venerable Priests, venerable by their age, and still more by their pure and blameless and fervent lives, officiated. They were concealed in our apartments with all that awful and anxious privacy which their own safety and our own prescribed. One of them, Father de Rosaire, a Dominican, the confessor of my mother for many years, about 78 years of age, with a head of snow-white hair, the calmest features I ever looked upon, the simplicity of a child in all his ways; the other, Father Pacific, somewhat younger, say 75, a Capuchin, once much revered in the order, and holding positions of authority and confidence—a man of higher talents than Father de Rosaire, and equal virtues. In that room they both slept and lived, and there also they offered up the Holy Sacrifice. Each morning, when they had finished their early private devotions and preparatory exercises, my mother having seen that all was ready, called the family together and led them to that sacred room ; one or two, only, left to keep watch and give notice in case of any alarm. For two years, or nearly two years, Mass was thus celebrated in that room, beneath the Chapel of the Parliament House, then utterly profaned and made a den of thieves, being a part of the Bureau of the Revolutionary Committee. At one time indeed turned, if possible, to a still worse purpose, for one of the three Tribunals which supplied the Guillotine with victims took possession of it and for a while profaned the sacred name of Justice, within those walls where the divine Sacrifice had been so often celebrated. All the ornaments which marked its sacred use were profaned and broken down, so that scarce a trace was left of its original purpose. Afterwards, in better times, they were replaced and the Chapel again used as before the Revolution. The room beneath, so sacred in our eyes on account of the mysteries there celebrated, and as being the hiding place of those two holy confessors, was afterwards my room. I slept in it in 1815, when I again visited my mother for a few days, and as I write the memories which then thronged my mind return again, of those good Fathers in particular, who blessed my youth, blessed my family, in those dark days.

Mr. Bouvet.

Mr. Bouvet was an old merchant, retired from business and leading a pious life, half separated from the world, still enjoying every day at his house the company of some friends, long accustomed to visit there without disturbing his particular habits and exercises of piety. Amidst his practices was that of a few moments' retreat and spiritual consideration or reading, alone, some time after dinner. He withdrew for a while, then returned kind, serene, polite, amiable to all; used to that momentary absence, they did not mind it. The regularity of its duration, as determined in his little rule, secured his presence with punctual appearance. One day, however, he remained absent much longer than usual; they grew uneasy at the difference—waited awhile more—then yielding to some fear that he might be indisposed, they went up-stairs to his apartment, and to the closet; their rap was not answered—nor a second—nor a call aloud by his name—Mr. Bouvet! . . . . they entered—the good man was sitting in his arm-chair, his head gently dropped on the breast—his two hands upon the page of a quarto book opened and resting on his knees—the book of the City of God, of St. Augustine, opened at the very chapter on the happiness of Heaven. He read; he died; he went to see and enjoy.

Thus did Mr. Boursoul die in the pulpit of the Parish of All Saints in Rennes, preaching on the happiness of Heaven, and repeating from time to time through the discourse his text, " We shall see Him as he is." At a last and most earnest repetition of the blessed words he dropped his hand on the pulpit, his head on his breast, a long pause—they thought it merely a pause!—it continued too long; they hastened to the pulpit—the spirit had fled. " He spoke of Heaven," said a boy in the congregation, " lo! he has gone thither!"

After the terror of 1793, the Priests who had prevaricated and taken the guilty oaths, often made their retraction and did public penance, many with marks of lively sorrow for their scandals. One of them at Grenoble did it with such a degree of compunction that, after having spoken a while with increasing fervour, he actually yielded to his grief and died in the pulpit in that act of his exemplary penance.

JOURNAL.

THE leaves of Bishop Bruté's Journal, preceding what immediately follows, had been torn out and destroyed, probably at some moment of particular alarm. The first part of what was left had also been torn out of the book, and is on loose leaves.

. . . .

The 1st Floreal[1] (20th April, 1795). The Chouans

[1] The Revolutionary Calendar was as follows :

AUTUMN—*Vendémaire*, or the Vintage month, from Sept. 22 to Oct. 21.
Brumaire, Fog month, from Oct. 22 to Nov. 20.
Frimaire, Sleet month, from Nov. 21 to Dec. 20.
WINTER—*Nivose*, Snow month, from Dec. 21 to Jan. 19.
Pluvoise, Rain month, from Jan. 20 to Feb. 18.
Ventose, Wind month, from Feb. 19 to March 20.
SPRING—*Germinal*, Sprouts month, from March 21 to April 19.
Floreal, Flower month, from April 20 to May 19.
Prairial, Pasture month, from May 20 to June 18.
SUMMER—*Messidor*, Harvest month, from June 19 to July 18.
Thermidor, Hot month, from July 19 to Aug. 17.
Fructidor, Fruit month, from Aug. 18 to Sep. 16.

All the public acts of the French nation were dated according to this system for a period of more than twelve years. It commenced from the 22d September, 1792, which is marked as the first year of the French Republic. It continued until the 10th Nivose, an XIV (31st Dec., 1805), when Napoleon restored the Gregorian Calendar. Few things marked more strongly the mingled folly and impiety of the whole affair than this new computation of time.

having signed a Treaty of Peace, at the Mabilais, the Representatives and Generals left Rennes at 2 o'c. to go and meet them. A large crowd accompanied them. About 7 o'c. in the evening a discharge of artillery announce their entrance. Among other Chouans, in company with the Republican generals Krieg, Hoche, Hombert, and the representatives, were Cormatin, Bunel, Dufour, De Jarri, Belle-vue and Bois-hardi, and about a dozen others, comprising their servants. Cormatin marched at the head of the procession, with a branch of Laurel in his hand, crying out from time to time, *Vive la Paix, la réunion, les bons Français*, but no Vive la République. From the Hospital to the Hôtel Châteaugiron the streets were lined on both sides with troops and national guards. Some few persons shouted *Vive la République*, the chief cry was *Vive la Paix*, but even this without enthusiasm. A dinner had been prepared for them, but it turned out to be a supper, for they did not sit down to table until half-past 8 o'c. The public were admitted to the dining hall in such numbers that the dinner was served with much difficulty. There were about forty at table, fifteen of them Chouans, wearing the cockade, and several of them with feathers in their hats. There were no healths drank, and nothing remarkable occurred. I came away about 10 o'c., and at half-past 10 all was over.

Monday, 18th of May. Messrs. Cormatin, De Jarri, and Duteilleul made a complaint to the department that since the Treaty of Peace more than 150 officers and soldiers had been killed; that the Republican soldiers worried the peasants with all sorts of exactions, and ill-treated them on account of their refusal to wear the tricolor cockade, a matter upon which even the Representatives had shut their eyes, knowing that they would never be able to get the country people to wear an emblem under which so many atrocities had been committed, any more than they could be made to look with favour upon those who had become possessed of Church property, and had carried arms to vex and injure them.

A member complained that they were still disarming.

Mr. Cormatin replied that this was a consequence of the mistrust which the farmers and country people entertained of those who had oppressed them and taken away their crops, but that it was not done by his orders, and that he would endeavour to have the arms returned.

They agreed to confer together often, and to make known their complaints on both sides.

Monday, 25th May. The Monday after Pentecost Sunday it was whispered about that they intended to arrest the Chouan leaders. Among others, Launai, the keeper of the *Tour de Bat*, said in the presence of several persons, among others of ——, that before evening he would have Cormatin undergoing his Purgatory. —— immediately made this known to the Chouans, but they would not believe that there was any danger. Cormatin in fact passed almost the whole day with the Representative Bollet, who had arrived the evening previous.

About 6 o'c. in the evening they arrested Cormatin; Solhillac, Dufour, Julie, La Nonée, and 33 others were arrested at the Grande Maison and conducted to the *Tour de Bat.* At 8 o'c. another guard went to the Grand Maison, with Mr. Guezon, Judge of the Peace, and put a seal upon all their papers; at 9 o'c. Mr. Boisgoutier was arrested. At midnight they went to the house of Mr. Poutigni, but did not find him. The same night all the prisoners, together with Kuen, who, being at the Grande Maison at the time of their arrest, was arrested with them, started for the Island of Pelée, near Cherbourg, under a guard of 800 men.

The same evening a battalion was sent to surprise the camp at Cicé. The accounts are so contradictory that I do not know what occurred there. The report is that the troops of the battalion fired upon those in the encampment, but that they escaped and crossed the river. The next morning a carriage, containing a volunteer and two wounded Chouans, came to the Unity Hospital; they say that some persons were killed on both sides. In the afternoon the battalion returned, bringing with them eight men, four women, two children, and a little girl. They marched their prisoners through the principal streets of the city before shutting them up in the Tour de Bat. About half-past six in the evening another company arrived, bringing Mr. Dugueslin (St. G***) and M. the Rector of Montauban ; I do not know why they have arrested the Rector. During the night they brought Mr. Bunel du Grand St. Meen, and the next day Mr. Pontavice du Fougeres.

The next day a Proclamation was posted up declaring all these persons guilty of Treason.

The war has begun again.

Thursday, 28th of May. The Municipality has given notice that a large body of troops are about to arrive. The Couriers from Brest and Dinan have been stopped by the Chouans. They gave the Courier from Dinan a discharge or receipt, signed *Moustache* and *La rejouissance.*

Friday, 29th May. The 72d regiment arrived here to-day from Belleisle, and a large number of other troops. Kuen arrived here this evening, having been set at liberty.

Saturday, 30th May. Mr. Pontavice has been set free. They brought here M. de Bedée, son of the Marquis de Bedée, who was put to death, and with him one man and three women.

Wednesday, 3d of June. To-day they imprisoned Lenai, Blaise, &c., members of the former Committee.[2]

Friday, 5th of June. M. Bunel was let out of the *Tour le Bat* this evening. This afternoon they killed three Chouans near Montfort, and brought five more here as prisoners. They say there has been quite a sharp skirmish at Liffré, and that the Territorial Guard suffered severely.

Saturday, 6th June. Everything is very dear in

[2] The following list will give some idea of the character of the persons who climbed into power at this time, especially in the provincial towns. I found it on a sheet of paper among Bp. Bruté's manuscripts, copied apparently from some contemporary work:

Extract from the Journal of the Laws, and of the French Republic, by G. F. Galetty. Descriptive List of the Members of the ancient Revolutionary Committee of Rennes.

LEVOT, vender of umbrellas, formerly a servant at Dinant, turned away for his rascality.

PORTAIX, wooden shoemaker, knows how to write his name.

AUBIN, a shoemaker, a violent and bloody man, who can neither read nor write.

OVNORIX, a poor barber.

MANELLA, formerly a German pastry cook, whose goods his wife and children have carried away to Switzerland, for safe keeping; a faithless man, at present director of the hospital, formerly St. Ives.

RIELLANT, worker in metals, a drinker of blood.

BELAISE, a hatter; in 1793 without a penny, to-day very rich; a great scoundrel, whose rascalities have been exposed in a printed memoir.

DUPIN, merchant tailor; a dupe, sometimes humane, and would be always so if he were less of a drunkard.

PELLANT, a shoemaker, as great a scoundrel as Carrier.

GOURVES, a tailor; a hard, fierce man, who has added to his property by stripping the gold off of vestments and articles of ecclesiastical life.

LA ROCHE, marble-worker; his heart is as hard as the stuff he works in, and the rock whose name he bears.

the market. To-day I had a conversation with M. Bunel and his son. M. Bunel told me that the evening before his arrest he received a letter from General Hoche, expressing the greatest satisfaction at his conduct, and requesting him to come hither, in order that they might confer together in regard to the pacification. The next day the Chouans who were in Rennes were arrested, and he at St. Meen.

NOTE.—The Republicans have several times broken the truce which was made on the 3d and 4th Floreal. Messieur Geslin and l'Hermilé were massacred near Laval; another day Allard was killed at Retiers—several others whose names I neglected to note down. I regret also that I did not preserve an article by Mr. Cormatin, in which he complains of eleven officers, 114 soldiers, and seven Priests having been put to death by the Republicans. I think that this number is somewhat exaggerated, but there can be no doubt that many were killed after the armistice. Some Republicans were also killed.

Friday, 12th of June. M. Chateaud'assis was brought here to-day and imprisoned; also in the afternoon the Rector of St. Jacut, and Father Loiseau, Jacobin of Dinan, who were never exiled. Kuen left here to-day.

Thursday, 18th June. Fifteen men and five children were brought in to-day—seized in their beds at Breal, as Chouans. There is a rumor to-day of the death of Boishardi, and the Dauphin.

M. Le Coz[3] came into the city with thirteen others of the same stamp, to make their declaration in regard to the decree of the 11th, and signed a circular of about a page, which the city refused to publish at its own expense. He caused prayers to be said for the recovery of Mr. Barbier, who is very ill.

Friday, 9th. The news of the death of the brave Boishardi is confirmed; killed 29th Germinal. He was Captain in the Regiment de Vaisseax.

Saturday, 20th. All sorts of provisions are dearer than ever; veal 80 to 100 francs the quarter.

Six couriers have arrived, who confirm the news of the death of Louis XVII. and the capture of Luxembourg.

Tuesday, 23d. We have news of B—— through P——; he is doing well. Four Chouans brought in to-day. Father Caillebat has retracted.

[3] Le Coz was the intruded constitutional Bishop of Rennes. He had been Principal of the College of Quimper and was elected by the people (?) under the new order of things in 1791. The true Bishop of Rennes at that time was Monsigneur Barean de Girac, eminent for his virtues and moderation, but who courageously resisted the intruder. Obliged afterwards to leave France, he became the friend and spiritual director of Stanislaus Poniatowski, the last King of Poland. He survived the Revolution and died Canon of St. Denis (having resigned his See at the time of the Concordat) in 1820, aged 86. Le Coz was one of the Constitutional Bishops forced upon the Pope by Napoleon at the time of the Concordat. He was made Archbishop of Besançon, and died in 1815. He was a man of irreproachable morals and considerable talent, but it was all made of no effect by his obstinate and exaggerated constitutionalism.

Thursday, 25*th*. Martin, the Carmelite, who took the civil oath and got married, made his retraction to-day before M. de la Croix and three witnesses, Messrs. Blouet, Caron, and Malenfruct. The constitutional Rector de Gahart also made his retraction a short time since. A form of declaration for the Priests to sign was brought to us this evening. It has been printed and circulated. Most of the Priests are opposed to signing anything of the sort. The Rector of St. Saviour thinks it might be well to sign a simple declaration to the following effect: "We declare that we have always been submissive to the laws, except in those points where they have been contrary to the Holy Roman Catholic and Apostolic Religion, and that we have always endeavoured to promote peace and concord amongst the citizens. In faith of which," &c.

Friday, 26*th*. It was finally determined not to sign any declaration. Mr. Cornue informed me that Coz, in making his declaration, excepted the law of divorce—the marriage of Priests, and other similar points. A number of the *Emigrés* have made a landing at Quiberon, after a naval fight, when the English fleet captured three of our vessels.

Saturday, 27*th June*. To-day the municipality posted up its invitation. There has been a tumult, occasioned by a large crowd of people who assembled on hearing that the churches are to be shut up to-morrow. They marched to the City Hall, and were sent by the Municipality to the Representative, who gave them a letter addressed to the Mayor; but a large number of young men, with drawn sabres, were posted before his residence, and in the confusion the letter was lost.

Sunday, 28th. This morning another crowd assembled about the residence of the Representative; their leaders were not permitted to speak, and a patrol seized two of the ringleaders; from thence they went to the Hôtel de Ville; the members of the Municipality were at the windows, and the door was guarded by soldiers without arms, and a number of young men. The Mayor came and addressed them, but no one could tell exactly what he said. When he had withdrawn, the soldiers and women commenced fighting with their fists and with stones. The women were obliged to retire, but not without giving the Municipality a piece of their minds, and loading them with all sorts of maledictions. A few of the most rebellious remained scattered here and there, who were treated shamefully by the soldiers —who even went so far as to flog two of them in the alley de Burnel, under the very eyes of the Municipality. At length General Krieg came and reprimanded the soldiers very severely, and calmed the people, so that by 11 o'c. all was quiet. In the afternoon they assembled at the College, to sign petitions to demand the provisional exercise of worship; a committee of twelve was appointed to obtain signatures in the different communes: the two Mademoiselles Duparc, Mademoiselles Dusselainée, Gerbier Jouanin, Hipolite Michel, Joffe, Le Tissier, Robert, St. Trimoi, Le Vicomte, La Sauvelaye. They waited upon the Representative, who said that he would send their petition to the Convention, but that he could not decide anything definitely himself.

Monday, 29th. During the forenoon nothing was done, but in the afternoon the above mentioned committee presented letters to each of the constituted authorities, those of the Department, the District and the City, requesting them to give their support to the petition which had been forwarded to the Convention. They were but coldly received; but they tried to cover up the matter, as well as they could, in order to quiet the people, to whom they said that the answer had been deferred until Wednesday. From 15 to 20,000 signed the petition before they ceased obtaining signatures.

This evening they brought in under arrest ten suspected Chouans; one of them thus arrested was a nephew of Mademoiselle Vatar, who, going on a visit to Mr. Buret, happened to be without a passport; the others were seized at a dance at St. Jacques.

Tuesday, 31st. Orders have been issued for cutting away the bridges, &c.

Wednesday, 1st July. About 6 o'c. in the evening large numbers assembled at the College; the committee or commissioners above mentioned were there, and twelve gentlemen were added to the commission: Messrs. Varin, Colum, Blouet, Malenfaut, Destrieux, L'Hermitage, the brother of Mr. Guignard, Rapulet, two gentlemen from the country, and three others whom I did not know. Whilst they were assembled, a rumor was circulated that the Mayor was coming, and to show the disposition of the people, one of the speakers declared that if the Mayor did come, and require them to submit to the present state of things, their unanimous declaration would be, "We will not." But he did not come.

Thursday, 2d. On Thursday at 2 o'c. the Clergy met together at M. de Romilley's and drew up their declaration, which was presented to the Department by a committee of five, viz.: Messrs. De Romilley, Dom.-Jehors, Rihet, Touchet, La Croix. It was accepted, and the commissioners very civilly treated. The people were at first afraid that by thus acting the Clergy would be confounded with those who had taken the oath, but were reassured by the explanations given to them. They commenced by putting the church in order, at the college, which had been entirely despoiled. The people chanted the Te Deum, Hymns to the Blessed Virgin, &c. The day after they had High Mass.

Saturday, 4*th*. A quarter of veal sells for 150 francs.

Thursday, 7*th*. Bladet and Tallien, the Representatives, have arrived with full powers.

Friday, 8*th*. We have news that the English have captured nine ships and a corvette near St. Malo.

Friday, 10*th*. The Republicans have been defeated at Mordelle. In the afternoon a courier announced the defeat of Hoche, with the loss of part of his artillery.

Sunday, 25*th*. Over one hundred children made their first communion at the Carmelites; many of them children of Republicans.

Tuesday, 27*th*. The diligence from Normandy was attacked, the escort defeated, and two of the passengers killed.

Wednesday, 28*th*. Dorvo has been assassinated by the Chouans at his country-house; his brother was killed last March. It was he who purchased the Presbytery at St. Aubin and other ecclesiastical property.

Thursday, 29*th*. The Bishop of Dol (De Hercé) was shot, after the surrender at Quiberon. I have the details at fourth hand from General Hombert. When he was seized he said: "The misfortunes of war cannot dishearten a man whose heart is pure, and filled with a zeal for Religion." He made a speech before the military commission so touching that the soldiers were affected by it, and the Judge was obliged to silence him.

Tuesday, 2d Sept. Mr. Ginguené, who was arrested the 14th of August, was tried before the military commission, condemned and shot this morning, although he has been for a long time crazy, and had a certificate to that effect. When led out to execution, he had no idea where he was going, and said to the prisoners: "Good-by, my friends; I am going to take a little turn which will do me good."

Sunday, 7th. The Constitution has been accepted, even by the soldiers, to whom it was read the evening before—more favoured in this respect than the citizens, who knew nothing about it until the moment when it was proclaimed in the different sections.

Tuesday, 9th. The elections were held to-day.

Monday, 15th. 1500 troops arrived here to-day from Vitri. Eight Priests from the district of Dol, four from Barenger, two from Tremblai, and one from Marcillé, were brought here to-day, and although the Judge was obliged to acknowledge that they had been illegally arrested, they were put in prison.

Wednesday, 17th. The Department has published the Decree. Le Coz (the constitutional Bishop) went and took the new oath, renouncing the restrictions he made before, but declaring that he persevered in them mentally.

Thursday, 18*th*. Some persons asked permission of the Municipality to shut up the church, but they forbade it to be done.

Thursday, 29*th*. A column of troops and four pieces of artillery left to-day for the Convention, with the Representative Matthieu.

Sunday, 8*th Nov.*, 1795. Clermont has been killed at Mossac in an affair with the Chouans, who had the advantage and killed many of the Republicans. The Republicans abandoned the post the following day, and brought their wounded here.

Monday, 9*th Nov*. Matthieu arrived here to-day, and has called the Municipality to account for not enforcing more strictly the law against Priests. The Municipality answer him with firmness, but they will be obliged to make a show of compliance at any rate.

Thursday, 13*th Nov*. They commenced to-day making domiciliary searches. They are made by the Commissioners of Police, with an escort of Gendarmes. If they seize any one they are to be taken to St. Meen.

Saturday, 15*th*. The searches are finished. It so happens that no one was caught.

Monday, *Dec 2d*. The brother of Dupin has been killed.

Thursday, 5*th Dec*. Twelve men and women sent to Fougéres to be judged.

Saturday, 7th Dec. M. Dessolles de Condrai killed near the Hermitage. The two sons of the Farmer at the Maison Blance, on the road to St. Laurent, were assassinated.

Sunday, 15th Dec. Fifty-one men brought here from Vesin, arrested at Mass. Douazel escaped from St. Meen. Three persons, two of them Chouans, escaped from the Tower (Tour de Bat) and a Chouan Captain from the Grand Prison.

Thursday, 19th Dec. The Chouans seized a convoy near Mordelle and killed thirty men, about noon to-day.

Saturday, 20th Dec. The diligence has arrived from Paris; it was plundered of everything by a party of Chouans, who carried away even the horses.

Sunday, Dec. 21. Trial of forty-eight of those who were arrested at Vesin; condemned to one month's imprisonment, and a fine of 100 francs each. The Priest was sentenced to ten years' imprisonment in irons.

Tuesday, Dec. 23d. A new General named Hedouville has arrived to replace Rey.

Wednesday, 25th Dec. Two young men from Pacé shot (fusillé).

1796, *January 2d.* A man from Cuillé shot—the father of five children. A convoy has been taken by the Chouans at St. Merial and forty men killed.

Saturday, 9th Jan. The Chouans have taken

Combourg. [This was the Château of the Châteaubriands, of which M. de Châteaubriand has given so interesting an account in his Mémoires d'Outre Tombe.]

Tuesday, 12*th Jan*. The Curé of Bruz, M. Le Pé, was brought from Bruz to St. Meen. Guillopé, a Captain of Chouans, has been arrested and imprisoned at Montfort; he is wounded.

On the margin of this entry in his Note Book Bp. Bruté wrote, apparently when reading it over many years afterwards: "Poor Guillopé—he was an excellent student in my class—very strong and robust, but of the mildest disposition; we were intimate friends."

Under the date of *Saturday*, 30*th February*, he writes: "Guillopé was shot to-day at Montfort; when taken he was covered with wounds."

Friday, the 15*th Jan*. The Chouans who were taken yesterday were brought before the General to-day, viz.: Mouillenaise, 24 or 25 years of age, Chief of the Canton of Ille and Vilaine; Rallé, 18 years of age; Le Crochair, called l'Avocat, 25 to 30 years old, from St. Malo, Chief of the Maar; Applagnac, about 50 years of age, nephew of Mr. Satre, Chief of the Canton of Liffré. They were imprisoned in the *Tour le Bat*. At 6 o'c. they were brought before the Tribunal; there were not twenty citizens present, except a guard commanded by Balland and Audoin; the Hall was full of soldiers.

Ponsard, who said that he came to defend Rallé, denied the competency of the Tribunal, and Le Crochair proved in the most evident manner that, according to the laws, especially that of the 1st Vendémiaire, the court was incompetent to try them. The Judge, however, overruled them and ordered the trial to proceed; at two hours after midnight they were condemned to death, except Rallé to 25 years in the Galleys. When they had returned to the prison, they asked for a Priest to hear their confessions, and the General, having been consulted, granted their request, and Mr. Rolandier, Curé of Beaucé near Fougéres, who had been brought from Vitré to the Grand Prison, was sent to them. On Saturday, about noon, they were led to execution by an escort of about 150 soldiers. They exhibited the greatest firmness; Applagnac, who was a strong man, about five feet seven inches tall, with a large moustache, had the most of a military air about him; their calm and steady bearing seemed to awe the crowd who surrounded them. They were shot in the meadow of Mt. Morin; their last words were "Vive le Roi et la Religion."

Wednesday, 20th Jan. The City declared to be in a state of siege by Giroust the Commissioner.

Friday, 29th Jan. The Chouans have captured a convoy near Mordelles, and seized 6000 packages of cartridges, with clothing, money, &c.; they killed and took prisoners sixty soldiers of the eighty who composed the escort.

Thursday, 4th Feb. They began to-day to arrest large numbers of young men.

Friday, 12th Feb. Two young girls condemned to death for having carried powder to the Chouans.

Saturday, 13th. Madame Bellevue from La Croix, Robert a hussar deserter, and a person named l'Ecrivain condemned to death.

Sunday, 14th. The five persons condemned on Friday and Saturday were shot to-day; a baker boy, who had got up into a tree to see the executions, was killed by one of the bullets.

Wednesday, 17th. Hoche arrived to-day; left on Saturday (20th) for Angers.

[I omit many particulars from the Journal, each day, filled up with accounts of skirmishes, arrests of Priests and others, searches, &c.]

Tuesday, 2d March. Four Priests, M. Briart, Rector of Moulin; M. Gaignart, Prior of Arbresec; M. Yvan, Canon of La Guerche, were brought here to-day from La Guerche, and put in prison at St. Meen.

Tuesday, 9th March. A detachment arrived from La Poterie bringing with them three hats, with white feathers, which they say belonged to three Chouan leaders, whom they killed.

Saturday, 22. It is reported that La Charette has been seized.

Easter Sunday. Radiguel shot.

Wednesday, in Easter week. Festival of Youth—only 18.

Friday, 29th April. My brother arrived this evening, and has been arrested.

Thursday, Ascension. Chef d'Or, leader of Chouans, shot.

Tuesday, 14th June. Madame Montluc and her children arrived this evening about 10 o'c. They are lodged at Crosco, with Madame La Gervesais.

Thursday, 16th June. At 2 o'c. this morning the Montlucs and Mademoiselle La Gervesais left for St. Malo, with a Passport from the Generals, to return to Jersey. M. de Montluc is at St. Malo to accompany them.

Sunday, 7th August. At the parade to-day the state of siege was declared raised.

September 25th. They have commenced demolishing the Church of St. Martin.

October 15. Hoche assassinated; Le Pottiere arrested the assassin, who is a workman at the Arsenal, and a man named Charles who hired him.

October 16th. The petition in favor of the Priests has up to Sunday exceeded 14,000 signatures.

October 31st. The Central School was opened to-day, with discourses by Malherbe, Beaugeard, Le Gravesend, and Rabillon.

November 12th. Five Priests escaped from St. Meen.

November 22d. Last night, 21–22, about 2 o'c., a fire broke out in the Faubourg L'Evêque, and burnt for two hours.

November 26th. An assassin was guillotined to-day; he wore a red robe.

December 15th. The Minister of Marine passed through the city to-day on his way to Brest.

December 20th. The courier who should have arrived here to-day was attacked near Alençon; a passenger killed.

December 24. The Priests let out of prison.

1797. *January 21st.* The anniversary of the King's death was celebrated by the firing of cannon and a parade of the troops and the National Guard, which numbered only 84 men. The only one who addressed them was Le Gravesend. The troops refused to cry "Vive la République" until they had been commanded to do so four times.

February 12th. The news of the taking of Mantua arrived this evening. [Mantua was surrendered to the French, January 7th, 1797.]

Feb. 19th, Sunday. The Te Deum was chanted in the Church of St. Saviour in honour of the Italian victories and the taking of Mantua. It was announced by a printed Circular, which they had the impudence to send to the principal persons among the Clergy who had refused the oath. [This celebration was under the auspices of Le Coz, the intruded constitutional Bishop.]

March 21, *Tuesday.* The elections commenced to-day.

March 23, *Thursday.* The elections ended. Many persons of extreme opinions, Terrorists and Republicans, protested against them.

May 7th, Sunday. Mr. Coz (the constitutional Bp.) had a first communion of the children of those who adhere to him. They say that there was only between one and two hundred. Large numbers also made their first communion in the houses of Catholics in the country Parishes, at Chautpie among others, more than 240.[4]

June 5, *Monday.* Mr. Rebulet (a non-juring Parish Priest), who had been about during the last week, officiated publickly yesterday, in the forenoon and afternoon. A large crowd of people attended—I was told upwards of 4000—who welcomed him with enthusiasm.

June 21*st, Wednesday.* The Department has published a decree restoring certain Churches to publick worship. St. Germain has been vacated by the troops; the College also. St. Aubin, which has been used to store hay, St. Hélier and St. Laurent have been reopened.

[4] On a loose slip of paper I find the following notes in Bishop Bruté's handwriting:

"Condition of religion at Easter, 1797. The Easter duty has been made by a large number of people. The Altars have been richly ornamented. On Thursday, the Paridises were superb—Vespers, &c. On Easter Sunday, at the Madelaine and S. Hélier, High Mass—Blessed Bread—Sermon—Solemn Vespers, as of old."

June 22, *Thursday.* They are working at the Churches. They are bringing articles from all sides for the use of the Churches; many articles which formerly belonged to them.

The parishioners of St. Aubin have sent a deputation to Mr. Coz, to request him to restore their Saints. [I presume some pictures or statues which he had taken away.] The Parish of St. George have requested "Le Bon Pasteur," but have been refused.

Friday, 23*d June.* The work on the Churches still continues. They make collections at the doors; écus and louis d'ors even are put into the box.

This evening the parishioners of St. Hélier went in procession to meet their old Pastor. They brought him back in triumph, carrying the Blessed Sacrament; he preached on the return from the captivity of Babylon, and gave the Benediction of the Blessed Sacrament. The Churches of St. Aubin and St. Germain reblessed. General Kling was present at the benediction.

They have posted up an order forbidding any more interments in the Cemetery of St. Hélier, because almost all are carrying their dead there.

Saturday, 24*th June* (St. John's day). High Masses were celebrated in all the Churches to-day; the crowd was very large at all the Masses; the first High Masses celebrated were at St. Hélier, by the Rector, who gave first communion to 120 children:

at St. Aubin by the Rector, who preached on the occasion; at the College by M. Rebulet, and at St. Germain by M. de la Croix. Everywhere there was a great concourse of people, so that they extended outside of the doors, into the street. There were soldiers, patriots, adherents of the constitutionalists, officials, and in fact all the most respectable families. The Blessed Bread (pain beni) was distributed.

At St. Germain a petition was read (Mr. Haie) asking for the recall of the Bishops and Priests exiled or emigrated; the parishioners were requested to sign it the following day, so that it might be sent to the Legislative Assembly. It was not read in the other Churches. Many Masses were also celebrated in private rooms.

It is noticed that Le Coz's church (the constitutional Bishop's) is rapidly falling off.

Sunday, 25th June. A notice from the Municipality has been posted up, forbidding the Clergy to make use of the churches for any other purposes than those connected with divine worship.

Wednesday, 28th June. The Festival of Agriculture was celebrated to-day without any enthusiasm [tristement].

The Municipality has forbidden the people to sign the petition which had been got up at St. Germain's, by Mr. Haie. In the evening some young men coming out of the Hôtel d'Artois, where they had been drinking to the health of Louis XVIII., fired upon the guard, who fired back, and arrested Morel.

Sunday, 2d July. Mr. Blanchard of the Petit Seminaire arrived here to-day from Spain. Mr. Durand and Mr. Halloche, condemned to transportation, were set at liberty.

Thursday, 5th July. A solemn service for the repose of the souls of all the Priests put to death during the Revolution was celebrated at the College.

Saturday, 7th July. Mr. Le Coz issued to-day a printed circular in regard to the convocation of a *Council.* He sent parcels of them to the different Churches, but they were sent back unopened.

Saturday, 22d July. A letter from Lanjuinais appeared on the Bulletin, in which he accuses Rennes and the authorities of being animated by an anti-revolutionary spirit—*d'esprit contre révolutionnaire.*

Tuesday, 25th July. The Municipality has addressed a very severe reply to Lajuinais, calling upon him to retract.

Sunday, 28th July. To-day they arrested a simpleton (un fou) who, after having cut down the *liberty tree* of the Jacobins, was about to do the same to the one planted in the *Place du Palais.* The Municipality issued a proclamation on the subject. They celebrated the 9th Thermidor (the fall of Robespierre). General Kliȩ pronounced a very moderate discourse, with even a religious tone about it.

There is much quarrelling between the returned Chouans (Chouans rentré) and the artillery-men; many wounded on both sides. Grimandiere (Chouan) wounded Bernis, gunner; La Voltais wounded another gunner named Verdrix.

Tuesday, 30*th July*. Coz and Lanjuinais left to-day to attend the *Council* at Paris

August 3*d*. Mr. De Boisteillul, deputy, arrived to-day in company with the Rector of Chatillon and the parish Priest of Orgerer.

August 6*th*. The eldest son of M. de St. Hilaire was wounded to-day by another Chouan, because he expressed himself against recommencing the *Chouanage*.

August 6*th*. The banns of marriage were published at S. Germain for the first time.

August 15*th*. The Journal *Chausseblanche* has announced for some time, and particularly in its number for to-day (No. 59), that they are attempting to renew the *Chouanage*. It speaks of assemblies near Becherel, of the purchase of arms, &c., and attributes it all to the Priests.

Picard made his retraction at the College.

The *terrorists* are signing a petition at the *Corps de Garde* thoroughly revolutionary in its character, and full of calumnies against the Priests. The Municipality is endeavouring to hinder any more from signing it.

NOTE.—The Revolution of the 18th Fructidor (Sept. 4th, 1797) having taken place, I was obliged to discontinue and hide this Journal. I have commenced another in the small book, marked *Livre de Banque*.

Thursday, 21 *Fructidor, An* 5 (7th Sept., 1797). This morning at the parade, Moreau read an account of the Revolution, which took place (s'est operée) at Paris the 18th Fructidor,[6] and which confirmed the rumors circulated yesterday evening. The courier arrived at 5 o'c. this evening, but would make no answer to the questions put to him; he had a package for Beaujard, within which was another addressed to the Department, containing printed Proclamations in regard to the conspiracy, &c.

Beaujard looks sad and embarrassed. Those whom they call *terrorists* are very much excited, and have a triumphant look. The news, as it becomes more certain, has spread consternation and alarm on every side, and seems to produce a feeling of discouragement rather than active indignation. Strong patrols have been formed for the night.

Friday, 8th September. Mademoiselle Pasquier, one of the most ardent supporters of the Constitutionalists, died to-day. She was attended in her

[6] The Revolution of the 18th Fructidor was a reaction of republicanism, or rather of the Revolution, against the evident return to royalist principles. It was under the immediate guidance of Barras, but its real author was Napoleon, who foresaw the end of his ambitious schemes if the Royal family were restored.

last moments by Mr. Le François. Since the zealous Lanjuinais and Coz went to Paris there has been a great falling off from their party. The churches are open and filled with people, but alarm is marked upon every face. At St. Aubin a man walked into the church, during the service, with his hat on, evidently with the intention of insulting those who were worshipping there.

Saturday, 9th September. This evening the courier, whose coming has been looked for with so much impatience, arrived. He brought none but the most ultra republican papers; they contain the famous Law of general security (loi de sûreté générale), which violates so many articles of the Constitution.

Sunday, 10th September. At 5 o'c. this morning all the churches were shut up. The High Altar of St. Germain was only finished and dedicated on Friday.

The famous Law was enregistered to-day. Audoin gave Mr. Thibout a slap in the face, on the Place d'Armes, because he did not wear a cockade; several persons who were present seemed much pleased at the insult, and took no measures to hinder or repair it.

Monday, 11th September. The Priests who have taken the oath (to the civil constitution of the clergy) went to the Municipality to-day, to the number of fourteen, to take the new oath which is required.

The *Fathers of the Council* have taken it at Paris. The Courier of this evening brings the appointment of three new Judges. Langé preserves his place; Poignaut, who is a man of great merit, and universally esteemed, and Robion, are replaced by Leminihi, Jr., and Jourdain.

Saturday, 16*th September*. A Letter of the pretended *Council*, signed by Coz, President, and Lanjuinais, Secretary, printed at the office of the *Chausseblanche*, inviting the Bishops and Priests, who have refused to take the oath, to open negotiations for a reconciliation.

Tuesday, 19*th Sept*. They are taking up a collection among the "Terrorists" for a grand dinner, to be given on the 1st Vendémiaire. They are already making preparations in the large Hall (i. e. of the Parliament House, in which Madame Bruté occupied apartments).

Wednesday, 20*th September*. An order has been given to arrest any Priest found discharging the functions of his office, but they do not look for them.

Friday, 22*d September*. The Feast was given today. See Bulletin de *Chausseblanche* for details, No. 80. Beaujard made a very revolutionary speech; it was so bitter against the Priests, *cette caste abominable*, as he called them, that the moderate republicans took offence at it. Almost all the soldiers got drunk.

Sunday, 23d September. A report is in circulation that all the Priests are to be arrested.

Tuesday, 25th September. General Rouland was divorced to-day from his wife before the Municipality.

Sunday, 8th October. The Courier brings news to-day that the municipality has been turned out of office; this news has afflicted all honest people.

Saturday, 14th October. Proclamation of the new Municipality, in which they declare their devotion to the Republic and their attachment to moderate principles.

Sunday, 15th October. This morning a handbill appeared upon the walls, on which five of the Municipality were hung in effigy.

Monday, 16th October. The two Commissioners of Police have been turned out of office, and are replaced by L'Hartel and Chevet, ex-Jacobin monk.

Sunday, 22d October. To-day they celebrated a Festival in memory of General Hoche; his bust was carried in procession, speeches made, &c.

Saturday, 28th October. A Proclamation from Beaujard has been published, ordering the arrest of all suspected Priests, and those who are subject to transportation.

Monday, 30th October. At half-past 6 o'c. this morning they commenced a very rigid search after the Priests. They arrested only five, who were conducted to St. Meen, where they were placed in solitary confinement; on bread and water: Father Gilles, the Minim; Pichou, Parish Priest of St. John; La Gresillomaie; Renaud and Dufeu, all over sixty years of age, and some very infirm.

This evening a Courier arrived bringing news of the peace with the Emperor. This courier announced also the arrival in Brittany of an army for England, which is to be commanded by Buonaparte (le courrier annonce aussi l'arrivée d'une armée d'Angleterre en Bretagne, qui Buonaparte commandera).

They have arrested a Priest from Normandy, who has been living as a clerk with Mr. Petitpain the merchant. It was an apostate from his own country who recognized and denounced him to the authorities.

[This was Mr. Delaitre, of whom an account is given pp. 168–9 of the Sketches.]

Wednesday, Nov. 8th. The Priests imprisoned in St. Meen are kept in very rigorous confinement, are not permitted to walk in the garden, or hold any intercourse with those outside.

The niece of Mr. Massiot, Curé of Saint Hélier, has returned from Fontenay le Compte, where she went to visit him, but he was not there, having been transferred to Rochefort, to be transported with fifteen of his fellow Priests. The guard who conducted them to Rochefort robbed them of everything they had. They took away 400 francs from Mr. Massiot.

Sunday, 26th Nov. The (Ch. at the) College and St. Aubin opened to the Constitutionalists—two low Masses at each church—about 100 persons present.

Mem. Several apostate Priests were present at the divine office—some even who had married. They and the constitutional Priests fraternize, and walk in the streets together.

Wednesday, Nov. 29. Reboul, ex-Chouan, condemned to death for having killed persons before the month Pluviose, the year 4th of the Republic: after the sentence was passed he wrote a Letter in which he declared that if he had known that he was to be called to account for things done before that period, he would have died with his weapons in his hands; that he had done nothing since he gave up his arms. This makes the eighth condemned lately, almost all ex-Chouans.

What is most revolting is the outrageous language and conduct of the persons present; the sanguinary dispositions they exhibited surpasses belief, especially the women and old persons.

Friday, 15th Dec. A large number of persons arrested and conducted to prison from all parts of the city. The orders come from the Minister of Police at Paris.

Wednesday, 20th Dec. The Bulletin (Nos. 123 and 124) gives a list of those arrested; it is not complete. There is a curious article in the Bulletin inviting the inhabitants of Rennes to assist in opening a temple for worship, purified from old superstitions. They are to have hymns and a lecture, and an altar on which they are to offer fruits, flowers, &c. Le Coz, I am told, preached a furious philippic last Sunday against apostate Priests.

Saturday, 30*th*. First Decadi, celebrated by planting three liberty trees; nobody seemed to take any interest in the matter.

The principal peasants from D'Augné came to demand that their Parish Priest should be set at liberty. Several of those arrested have been let out of prison. Some refused to go out, and claim a trial, declaring that the *Constitution* has been violated in their regard.

Sunday, 21*st January*, 1798. The anniversary of the King's death celebrated with great ceremony; there were several inscriptions over the new *Calvaire* which they inaugurated the other day under the name of the "Temple of Peace." One was, "To hate Kings is to obey the Eternal." Another, "Anathema to Rome and England."

Saturday, 27*th Jan*. The ladies who take care of the Hospital of the Incurables [see Sketches, pp. 207–12] were brought up and reprimanded; they replied with much firmness that they had no Priest in the house, but that respectable persons came to visit the sick, and bring them some delicacies, and they often went into the chapel to pray.

Saturday, 10*th Feb.* General Desaix passed the night here on his way to the coast.

March 16. The division of the army of Italy, called "the terrible," and which has committed so many excesses on its route, particularly at Laval, arrived here to-day; the National Guard went out to receive them; they were feasted by the municipality.

March 18. The division left for Nantes.

March 21*st.* The primary assemblies held.

March 23*d.* Much confusion at some of the primary assemblies; the municipality sent soldiers to protect the *terrorists,* who found themselves likely to be outnumbered by the moderate and decent people. The soldiers drove out "les gens honnêtes."

August 8*th.* A general search throughout the Department; here it was commenced, in *violation of the Constitution,* at midnight. Among others they searched the houses of Messrs. Jouin Dulerain, father and son; De La Benneraye, De Blassac Destullaie, Le Sormel, Jauzé, Cohan, Sillardine, Rapetal, Monnier, La Massue, Du Plessix, La Croix, Tellier, De Cognac; of Mesdames Rebulet, De Bedée, &c., Mademoiselles Godard, Ergault, &c. &c. They found nothing.

August 21*st.* Many Priests arrested in the country and brought here. At 10 o'c. last evening, they gave notice to a number of Priests in the prison to get ready to start for Rochefort, which was easily done, as they had nothing in the world, and at 4 o'c. this morning they left, chained together two by two.

22d October. M. de le Neuville, *émigré*, was put to death (*fusillé*) to-day.

20th November. There was a terrible quarrel in the streets to-day, between the Grenadiers who arrived yesterday and the inhabitants; two or three killed on both sides, and several badly wounded.

December 15th. Joseph Sorette killed in the country. [This was the good Priest mentioned in the Sketches.]

December 16th. The Department has given the Bishop's house to an association who petitioned for it a short time since; they propose to establish there a literary and scientific society. Dauthon, Professor of Natural History, is the principal promoter of the plan; Rozais, Prof. of Physics; Thebaut, Prof. of Mathematics; Rabillon, Prof. of History; Lanjuinais, Prof. of Legislation; Tual, Physician; Duval, Duforneau, &c.

February 10th, 1799. William Duval killed.

Mem. I went to Paris this year, 1799, and ceased to keep a Journal of matters at Rennes.

Germinal, 11, 1801. Mademoiselle de Cicé brought to trial for the affair of the 3d Nivose.

27th. Collin acquitted of any accompliceship in the affair of the 3d Nivose, but condemned to three months' imprisonment and a fine of 300 francs for not having made a declaration to the Police.

25 *Fructidor.* Visited Collin at St. Pelagie.

15 *Ventose.* Present at the Corps Legislatif at the presentation of the Concordat.

21st. Entry of the Legate (Card. Caprara) into Notre Dame. Consecration of Monsig. Bernier, Pancemont and Cambacérès.

18 *Floreal.* The Senate reëlect Buonaparte for ten years. Buonaparte desires that the people should be consulted.

20th. Order of the Consuls, signed by Cambacérès, proposing the question—"Napoleon Buonaparte sera t'il consul a vie?"

3 *Thermidor.* Xavier Bichat died this morning at 4 o'c., 31 years of age, enjoying the very highest reputation in his profession and giving the greatest promise for the future; all his pupils loved him. His father and mother were most excellent people, very pious, and brought him up in the most Christian manner. When he first came to Paris he lived with his aunt, Madame Bouisson, and was very regular in the practice of his Christian duties; but afterwards, when he went to live with Dessant, he became careless. Dessant's widow, with whom he still lodged when attacked by his last sickness, watched with the greatest care to keep him from

seeing a Priest; but yesterday evening the Abbé Pinlibert, his former confessor (and who had been so zealous in assisting the persons guillotined during the reign of terror), made out to get to his bedside, and gave him absolution, in extremis. Bichat, however, never gave in to the reigning impiety, and was unimpeachable in his morals; but he was led away by his love of science and reputation. Let us pray to God for the repose of his soul. [This was the celebrated Physician of that name.]

18 *Fructidor*, 5*th Sep*. 1802. This morning at half-past 6 o'c. I was called in great haste to my aunt (Saulnier-Vauxelle); I found her insensible; when I called her name, she opened her eyes, but expired two minutes after my arrival. On Saturday, the Curé of St. Roch, who had been her friend and director for upwards of thirty years, heard her confession, and on Sunday night at 5 o'c. in the morning he gave her the viaticum and extreme unction. She was born in 1740—a Sister of Charity since 1758. She was possessed of a warm, generous heart, very firm in her character, a good administrator, entirely devoted to her duties—she loved her holy vocation, grieved over it when it was taken away, and hastened to resume it the first moment it was in her power—the most disinterested creature—never seemed to think of herself, refused all personal conveniences, always animated by a spirit of faith and confidence in God, which

was never weakened in the worst of times. Her nephew, Lisineau, Mazois, Jr., my friend Parrier, and myself attended the funeral; also four members of the *Bureau de Bienfaisance*, deputies from the 12 houses of Sisters in Paris, of whom the four oldest held the four corners of the Pall—besides these many friends of hers whom I did not know, and quite a crowd of poor people. The High Mass of requiem was sung at St. Roch. Her Sisters and ourselves accompanied the body to the Cemetery of Montmartre. The *De Profundis* was chanted in the church, and the Vicar made a short but admirable funeral discourse. She was buried at the north of the church, near the wall, among some tombs. *Requiescat in pace.*

6, 7, 8, 9 *Vendémiaire.* Examination and Concursus in writing for the prize. Examiners: Sabbatier, Lassus, Deyeux, Leclerc, Boyer.

23 *Vendémiaire.* Was examined. Examiners: Desgenettes, Petit Radal, &c.

3 *Brumaire.* Examination continued—Pinel, Richard, Sabbatier, &c.

5 *Brumaire.* Received the first prize, which I gave to my master and teacher, Mr. Duval, in recognition of his kindness; dined with my friends Buisson, Fizeau, Maisoneuve, Frain, Parrier, Villeneuve.

11*th.* Left for Rennes.

9*th Nivose.* Returned to Paris.

9th Pluviose. Collin let out of St. Pelagie, with an order to go to Nantes, and from thence to be exiled to the Isle of France. I went security for him.

On Easter night, 1803. Julien Duplessix, of Rennes, died in my arms at midnight, after 17 days' illness—19 years of age. Student in the Polytechnique School; studious, intelligent, amiable, loved by his fellow-students, a pious and faithful child of Mr. Delpitz. Mr. Carron has given a sketch of his life, 1815.

2 *Floreal.* Offered the situation of Physician to the 1st Dispensary; Parrier named Surgeon to the *Maison de Force.*

1 *Floreal.* Yesterday, Thursday, saw our Bishop at Passy, who approved of my intentions.

27 *Messidor.* Went to Rennes.

Fructidor. Montaux killed in a duel at Paris.

Ventidore an XII. Heard the news of the death of Mr. Châteaugiron, in London, 31st of last August—my old Professor and good friend. Exiled during the persecution; I have his portrait.

2 *Brumaire.* The eldest Mademoiselle Châteaugiron died this morning (I have worn her Chapelet about my neck ever since 1818).

21 *Brumaire.* Confirmation at St. Mélaine; 800 children, small and big.

23. Started for Paris, with my brother Augustin; mother approves of my choice.

Frimaire 4. My first lessons at the Seminary under Mr. Montague, Prof. of Moral Theology at the Seminary of St. Sulpice, Rue Notre Dame des Champs, No. 1456.

13*th March*, 1804. Mr. Bourges de Blerye, Curé of the Cathedral, died to-day; formerly principal of the College. "He is a Saint in Heaven," writes my mother, "but it is an irreparable loss for our city and the Diocese; hundreds of *pauvres honteux* have lost their support, and multitudes, I may say, of poor children. Every one loved him. The Prefect sent three times a day to find out how he was, and called himself. The General Laborde called every day. He overworked himself; it was after 6 o'c. in the evening before he had finished his visits and confessions, and then he had his office to say, letters to write, and at 4 or 5 o'c. in the morning he was in the Confessional again, hearing the confessions of the children, &c., who had to go to work. When he came out of the pulpit last Sunday he said, 'That is my last work.'"

10*th October*, 1804. Entered regularly into the Seminary of St. Sulpice.

25*th Nov.* Monsig. De Maillé, Bishop of Rennes, died this evening, 5 m. after 5 o'c. I received his last sigh and closed his eyes.

10. Appointed one of the clerks to serve Card. Fesch's Mass at the Tuileries, before Buonaparte.

18. Presented to the Holy Father (Pius VII.) M.

Champion's books and his letter in regard to the re-establishment of the Society. He raised his eyes and hands to heaven and said "Faxit Deus." How precious a remembrance that interview!

1806. Sœur Bonne died at Rennes—mother's dear friend—Superior of the Daughters of Charity at Rennes. Always chose the hardest and most disgusting tasks for herself. [See Journal, p. 208.]

1807. Made a collection to assist Mr. J . . . . . M. Pied de Nogent gave me 100 francs. Lord Shaftesbury, who was at that time at Paris with the Duchess of Devonshire, sent me 240 francs, through his friend Mr. Nicholas McCarthy, to assist this poor Seminarist. He had seen the Seminarists at St. Sulpice in the Parish Church, and in giving this money to Mr. McCarthy, he said that he wished those angels to pray for him. He has an excellent heart, said Mr. McCarthy to me, very near the true Faith

NOTES ON SOME OF THE VENDEAN OFFICERS WHO WERE HERE DURING THE PACIFICATION.

CORMATIN is a small man, about 40 years of age, with an open, sparkling eye—speaks quickly and with much facility; he is looked upon as a man of decided talent. I have heard him speak several times; he spoke easily and with elegance, though some of his phrases were rather too high-sounding; in the discussions his answers were prompt and adroit. Activity out of doors is his rôle. The people loved him very much and had great confidence in him.[6]

BUNEL—General of the *Ille et Villaine.* I knew Mr. Bunel better than the others, having been in his company more than twenty times at Madame Savignac's (sister-in-law of Gohiers). He was a young man, a little over twenty years of age; small in stature, and much marked by the small-pox. He looks feeble, but has the reputation of being very brave (he is suffering at present under the effects of a wound, received in a severe fight). He is grave beyond his age, very civil, but cold and preserving a very serious and reserved air in conversation. He is also very active and constantly on horseback, notwithstanding his wound.

CHARLES or BOISHARDI, General in chief of the *Côtes du Nord,* has most the air of a soldier about him of any of them; of a good height, very strong and active, about 30 years of age, open countenance, with the appearance of a man very frank and loyal; very brave, of which he has given plenty of proofs, but without cruelty. Elizabeth found

[6] Cormatin's real name was *Desoteaux;* he was a native of Burgundy, and served as an aid-de-camp to the Baron de Viomesnil, in the war of the American Revolution. He was afterwards at Metz, with the heroic Marquis de Bouillé, and aided him in the attempt to save the royal family of France. He took the name of Cormatin, which was that of his wife, at the time he joined the insurgents in Brittany.

fault with him for having signed the treaty of peace. "There has been plenty of bloodshed," he answered, "it will be better if we can succeed without shedding any more." He said this with an air of sincerity and *bonhomie* which rendered it very touching, coming from his mouth. He is constantly with Hombert—is adored by his followers and feared by the nation.—NOTE. He was killed the 29th Germinal (16th June).

JARRI—Commander *du Côte de Guer*. A fine-looking man, brown complexion, with rather a severe countenance, and an air of hauteur about him —spoke little; they were much attached to him in his part of the country, particularly for the good order he maintained.

JULIE—Aid-de-camp of Cormatin. The finest-looking man among the Chouans; tall, with a noble figure.

VILLERS—A young man about 15 years of age—called himself Marquis, from Burgundy. They were taking him with others to Brest, to make a sailor of him, when he escaped and joined the Chouans. His manners were easy, and he was not wanting in talent.

CHANTEREAU—I was not acquainted with him; he was regarded as a good officer, but was discontented, or jealous of Cormatin.

BEDEE—A small-sized young man, about eighteen years of age, much loved by his Chouans.

DUGUESCLIN—I knew him and loved him more

than any of the rest, except Boishardi, having often met him and conversed with him at our neighbours'. There was a mildness and kindness of heart joined to a chivalrous spirit about him that was charming. His real name was St. Gilles and he was the brother of the lady of that name. He was loved by all who knew him; large stature, fine figure, spoke with ease and gracefully.

REPRESENTATIVES.

BOLLÈT—Sent here for the pacification; a harsh man, detested by all; left in June, 1795.

GRENOT—Came during the pacification; a nobody, according to common opinion; left 10th July, 1795, with Bailleul.

BAILLEUL—I knew him only by a very weak and shallow proclamation against the Chouans; left 10th July, 1795.

MATTHIEU—Came the first part of July; he was looked upon as a man of ability; spoke well, and was a good sort of man.

Cathedral of St. Francis Xavier, 1834.

APPENDIX.

THE following Proclamation, the original of which I found among Bishop Bruté's papers, will show how much progress Liberty, Equality, and Fraternity had made in France after three years' bloodshed. Upon it was written the following note:

Notez bien que c'est trois mois encor après la mort de Robespierre qu'on charge follement de tout—c'est lorsque Cambacérès & Boissi d'Anglas presidoient la Convention, &a.

LIBERTE, EGALITE, FRATERNITE.

GOUVERNEMENT REVOLUTIONNAIRE.

ARRETE du Représentant du Peuple Boursault, délégué près les Armées des Côtes de Brest & de Cherbourg, & Départemens y contigus.

REDOUBLONS d'énergie et d'activité, nos ennemis ne dorment pas & ils sont toujours prêts à profiter de la moindre négligence. Surveillons, & nous déjouerons tous leurs projets, toutes leurs intrigues, & ils seront confondus, & la Liberté triomphera.

Les malveillans cherchent toujours à se soustraire aux mesures prises pour déjouer leurs complots, ils abusent, égarent et fanatisent les bons habitans des campagnes ; ils trompent leur bonne foi, et des prêtres fanatiques, des nobles aristocrates y publient le désordre & l'assassinat au nom d'un Dieu de paix qu'ils voudroient rendre complice de leurs fureurs.

Il est temps de faire cesser les funestes effets de ces démarches insidieuses, de cette influence envenimée, & de rammener tous les Français aux vrais principes. Il en est temps encore dans ces contrées désolées ; l'énergie & l'amour de la patrie n'y sont encore qu'assoupis, réveillons les bons Citoyens, relevons-les de cet état de léthargie & éclairons les esprits abusés.

Les Représentans du peuple ont déjà pris divers Arrêtés bien propres à former l'esprit public dans les Communes de campagne ; ils ont ordonné la lecture des Loix & Bulletins de la Convention ; ils ont prescrit des Instructions pour les jours de décadi, & ont rendu les Autoritiés constituées responsables de toute négligence.

Mais ce n'est pas encore assez, il faut découvrir, il faut faire punir les ennemis intérieurs qui trompent & égarent le bon Peuple, qui parcourent les Communes pour les faire insurger, qui y font circuler des espions à gages qui ne sont munis d'aucun passe-port ni d'aucun titre justifiant ce qu'ils sont, d'où il viennent où ils vont & ce qu'ils veulent ; il faut détruire ces pestes publiques & mettre à même les habitans des Campagnes de connoître leurs amis et leurs ennemis, de goûter les bienfaits de notre révolution, & de se réunir à la grande famille. Il faut donc prendre des mesures salutaires, qui fassent démasquer les scélérats et tomber sur leurs têtes coupables la vengeance Nationale

En conséquence arrête ce qui suit :

Article Premier.

A compter du vingt Brumaire tous les Citoyens des campagnes seront obligés d'être pourvus d'une carte civique qui leur sera délivrée par les Officiers Municipaux des Communes qu'ils habitent, & qui sera renouvelée tous les deux mois ; il ne pourra en être délivré qu'à des Citoyens connus pour résider légalement & actuellement dans la Commune, à peine par les Officiers Municipaux d'être traités comme suspects, cette carte désignera le quartier de l'habitation.

II.

A compter de la même époque, aucun Citoyen ne pourra s'écarter de plus une lieue de son domicile sans être pourvu de passe-port, à peine d'être traité comme suspect ; ceux délivrés antérieurement au présent Arrêté sont déclarés nuls.

III.

Les Municipalités tiendront un registre exact, contenant les noms & le lieu du domicile des Citoyens auxquels ils auront délivré des cartes civiques, & un autre registre d'enregistrement des passe-ports.

IV.

Tout Citoyen qui donnera asyle à un particulier non muni de passe-port, sera réputé suspect & puni comme tel, & si c'est un Prêtre réfractaire ou un émigré; la Loi a prononcé la peine de mort.

V

Tout Citoyen des Campagnes qui ne sera pas muni de carte civique à l'époque portée en l'article premier sera traité comme suspect, sauf l'examen sa conduite.

VI.

Tous les Citoyens sont en état de surveillance, pour seconder les efforts des Autorités Constituées, & arrêter tous les gens inconnus, suspects ou malveillans non munis de passe-ports ou cartes civiques.

VII.

Ceux qui refuseront de prêter secours à celui qui aura saisi quelque individu mentionné en l'article précédent, seront traités comme suspects.

VIII.

Les Comités révolutionnaires dans les lieux où il y en a, & les Municipalités dans les lieux où il n'y a pas de Comité, recevront les personnes arrêtées & les envoieront dans le chef-lieu du Département, & dans les trois jours au plus tard, ils adresseront une expédition en forme des procès-verbaux au Représentant du Peuple.

IX.

Ceux qui auront arrêté des individus mentionnés en l'article VI., recevront des récompenses proportionnées à l'importance de chaque individu qu'ils auroient conduit aux prisons.

X.

Dans la décade de l'affiche du présent Arrêté les Municipalités seront des états des étrangers qui habitent dans leurs Communes depuis moins d'une année, de leurs habitans absens sans cause légitime et connue, et notamment des jeunes gens de la pre mière requisition qui ne sont point à leur poste, avec la date des départs & arrivées, & une note sur les opinions & la conduite de chacun d'eux.

XI.

Les Commandans des postes militaires concourront avec les Autorités Constituées à la surveillance de la police de sureté générale dans les campagnes; aucun Officier Municipal ne pourra se refuser à accompagner la force armée ayant des ordres pour faire des visites domiciliaires dans les maisons soupçonnées de recéler des personnes suspectes. Cette force armée sera toujours commandée par un Officier responsable de la conduite qu'elle tiendra.

XII

Les Adjudans-Generaux sont autorisés, en prévenant le Général-Divisionnaire, d'établir dans leur arrondissement, partout où la sureté générale l'exigera, des postes militaires, qui seront placés par préférence à l'ébranchement des routes & hors des habitations. Les postes seront chargés d'examiner rigoureusement tous les passe-ports des voyageurs & les cartes civiques des Citoyens des campagnes, & d'arrêter ceux qui n'en seroient pas pourvus.

XIII.

Les Autorités Constituées & tous les bons Citoyens sont requis, au nom de la Patrie, de donner aux Commandans Temporaires & autres Officiers supérieurs, qui les seront parvenir aux Commandans des postes, des notes & le signalement des individus errans dans les campagnes.

XIV.

Le présent Arrêté sera imprimé & affiché dans toutes les Communes, à la diligence des Agens Nationaux de Districts, chargés spécialement d'en surveiller l'exécution, & qui sont autorisés à le faire réimprimer.

A Rennes, le 23 Vendémiaire, l'an troisième de la République Française, une & indivisible.

BOURSAULT.

www.ingramcontent.com/pod-product-compliance
Lightning Source LLC
LaVergne TN
LVHW010226110826
845151LV00004B/1197

* 9 7 8 1 4 2 5 5 2 5 9 9 6 *